Performance Management

Other titles in the Briefcase Series include:

Performance Management

Robert Bacal

McGraw-Hill

New York San Francisco Washington, D.C. Auckland Bogotá
Caracas Lisbon London Madrid Mexico City Milan
Montreal New Delhi San Juan Singapore
Sydney Tokyo Toronto

McGraw-Hill

A Division of The McGraw·Hill Companies

1 2 3 4 5 6 7 8 9 0 DOC/DOC 9 0 3 2 1 0 9 8

ISBN 0-07-071866-0

Library of Congress Cataloging-in-Publication Data
Bacal, Robert
    Performance management / Robert Bacal
      p. cm.
    A Briefcase Book
    ISBN 0-07-071866-0
    HR5549.5.R3B285 1999
    658.3/125 21
    98041555
    Subjects: Employees—Rating of. Performance standards.

*This is a CWL Publishing Enterprises Book, developed and produced for
McGraw-Hill by CWL Publishing Enterprises, John A. Woods, President. For
more information, contact CWL Publishing Enterprises, 3010 Irvington Way,
Madison, WI 53713-3414, www.execpc.com/cwlpubent. Robert Magnan
served as editor. For McGraw-Hill, the sponsoring editor was Catherine
Schwent, the publisher was Jeffrey Krames, and the production supervisor was Suzanne W. B. Rapcavage.*

Printed and bound by R. R. Donnelley & Sons Company.

McGraw-Hill books are available at special quantity discounts to use as pre-
miums and sale promotions, or for use in corporate training programs. For
more information, please write to the Director of Special Sales, McGraw-Hill,
11 West 19th Street, New York, NY 10011. Or contact your local bookstore.

 This book is printed on recycled, acid-free paper containing a
minimum of 50% recycled de-inked fiber.

Contents

Preface

As you hold this book in your hands, somewhere a manager and an employee are meeting to discuss the employee's performance—a performance appraisal meeting if you will. Chances are the manager would rather be doing something else. Odds are the employee would rather be having multiple root canal surgery without anesthetic. What's more, for every manager who's sitting down with an employee to evaluate performance, there's a manager who's trying to figure out how to avoid doing it—to avoid filling out the forms, having the meeting, communicating about performance.

OK, so most people really don't like performance appraisals. Should we care? Should you care? Probably. We know that communication between manager and employee about performance is essential to increase productivity, improve staff morale and motivation, and allow coordination of each employee's work so it contributes to the goals of the company.

But many managers focus on the wrong things. They focus on *appraisal* rather than planning. They focus on a *one-way* flow of words (manager to employee), rather than dialogue. They focus on required *forms* rather than the *communication* needed for everyone to succeed. They focus on the *past* rather than the *present* and *future*. They focus on *blaming* rather than *solving problems*. As a result, what should be a cooperative effort between manager and employee, working together as a team, turns into an awkward, stressful process both parties try to avoid. Or into a meaningless paper chase that wastes time and energy.

It doesn't have to be that way. While many companies and managers simply aren't getting much value from the time they spend in performance management and appraisal, there are people out there who are reaping benefits from the process. How are they doing it? How are they making it work?

That's what this book is about. It's about reorienting ourselves—focusing on what organizations, managers, and employees need to succeed. It's about looking at performance appraisal and performance management as ways to engineer success for everyone. It's about understanding that performance management is a people process. It's about helping you learn how to communicate cooperatively with staff to improve performance.

This book is not about theory. It's about doing all the things that make performance management work.

Why Read This Book?

Chances are you aren't getting full value from whatever you're doing to manage performance. That's why I wrote this book.

First, we help you focus on why you need to manage performance. What do you gain as a manager? How do employees benefit? How does your company gain? Second, we help you figure out how to do it so it works. You'll learn the steps in the performance communication/management process. You'll learn how to turn it into a true dialogue. You'll learn how to turn even badly designed forms and procedures into something useful. And perhaps most important, you'll learn how to reduce the discomfort most people associate with performance management and performance appraisal.

Overview

The first three chapters in this book will help you understand where performance management fits into the broader scheme of things and the benefits of doing it well.

Chapter 1 presents an overview of the process, defines it, and explains the payoffs for managers, employees, and the organization. In Chapter 2 we tackle some of the challenges of performance management. You'll find out why so many people try to avoid it. You'll also find out what makes a performance management system work—and the consequences of systems that don't work. Chapter 3 discusses performance management as a system in which all of the parts must work together. We'll also relate performance management to other things in your company—to strategic planning, to discipline, and to training and employee development.

Once we've set the stage, we move on to doing it and doing it right.

Chapter 4 helps you prepare yourself and your employees for the performance management process. You need information to make it work. What information? I'll tell you. How do you prepare staff to work with you? I'll help you with that, too.

Chapter 5 deals with what may be the most important part of performance management—performance planning. You and each employee must determine what he or she is to accomplish, identify the bull's-eyes the employee will be trying to hit. You work together so you come to a common understanding.

Chapter 6 talks about ongoing performance communication. You cannot simply set performance targets and then wait until it's time for appraisals. That approach is deadly and guarantees failure. We'll present some options for formal and informal ways to communicate about employee performance during the year.

In Chapter 7 you'll find a process for gathering data, observing, and documenting. Performance management and appraisal should be based on more than just opinions. It should be based on facts and observations. I also talk about the need to document and to communicate about performance, so both you and the company have some protection from malicious or unfair legal action.

In Chapters 8 and 9 we consider the performance appraisal and review process. You'll find a discussion of the merits and pitfalls associated with rating systems, ranking systems, and objective-based systems. I'll help you understand how you can conduct the performance review meeting so it's cooperative and so you and the employee are on the same side.

There's hardly any point in managing performance unless you work toward improving it. What's done is done. We need to look to the future and work with employees so they can get better and better.

Chapter 10 talks about the performance diagnosis and improvement process. How do you identify the causes of performance difficulties? Where do you look? And how do you remove barriers to performance?

Sometimes managers need to take action with respect to employees who are consistently not meeting expectations. While performance management isn't used primarily for disciplinary reasons, it does play an important role in dealing with serious workplace problems and difficulties. In Chapter 11 we'll talk about progressive disciplinary actions and how to deal with those tough situations.

Chapters 12 and 13 talk about some interesting alternatives and variations in performance management. You'll find information on 360-degree feedback techniques and other innovative approaches. We'll also answer the most common questions managers have about the performance management process.

Chapter 14 returns us to the central theme—that performance management is about creating relationships and ensuring effective communication. It isn't about forms or judging or categorizing employees. It's about people. In this chapter we'll talk about specific skills and things you can do to make it work.

Finally, in Chapter 15, we'll pull it all together with a case study. You'll read about Acme Progressive and how the company used a performance management system so everyone gained.

We don't believe that it's possible to use a cookbook approach to performance management. There isn't one recipe that will work for everyone. It is possible, though, to provide the principles and actions associated with successful performance management so you can make it work for your staff and your company. By the end of this book, you will have a good grasp of the whys, hows, whens, and whats of performance management so you can develop a way of doing it that helps everyone—you, your staff, and your organization.

Special Features

The idea behind the books in the Briefcase Series is to give you practical information written in a friendly person-to-person style. The chapters are short, deal with tactical issues, and include lots of examples. They also feature numerous boxes designed to give you different types of specific information. Here's a description of the boxes you'll find in this book.

These boxes do just what they say: give you tips and tactics for being smart in how to help employees improve their performance.

These boxes provide warnings for where things could go wrong in the performance management process.

Here you'll find how-to techniques for assuring that the performance management process goes well.

Every subject has its special jargon and terms. These boxes provide definitions of various concepts important to understand in managing performance.

Want to know how others do it? These boxes provide examples that show effective performance management in action.

Here you'll find specific procedures you can follow to make it easer to plan and execute your performance management plan.

 How can you make sure you won't make a mistake? You can't, but these boxes will give you practical advice on how to minimize the possibility.

Acknowledgments

I would like to thank John Woods of CWL Publishing Enterprises for asking me to write this book. He and Robert Magnan, also of CWL, worked with me throughout its writing and helped make the book you now hold a reality.

This book is dedicated to two fathers, Peter Bacal and Stan Moore, who have passed on.

Also to the other "family": Allan, Sylvia, the two Brians, the two Martys, Nancy, Chris, and the rest of the Christmas Eve bunch, who for thirty plus years have taught me what it is like to be human. See you on December 24, 2025, in the old folks' home. I'll send you a rattle in the morning.

Performance Management: An Overview

It's year-end at Acme Progressive. Apart from wrapping up the accounting, managers and employees are going through their yearly dance of performance appraisal, as they call it.

Michael manages fourteen employees directly, so he's going to be busy meeting with each of them, filling out forms, and gulping antacid. Since the personnel department is pushing him to get his forms in on time, he has to figure out a way to get this all done as fast as possible.

And he does. He sends an appraisal form to each employee via interoffice mail. After employees complete the forms, he meets with each one for about fifteen minutes to discuss the forms, and then signs them. Voilà! Problem solved. The paperwork gets done on time, the personnel department is content, and everyone goes back to their "real work."

What's Wrong with This Picture?

The better question might be "Is there anything right with this picture?" Let me give you a bit more information about Acme.

Typically the forms that Michael and the other managers send on to the personnel department are put into file folders and mostly forgotten. The information on the forms is so vague and unreliable it can't be used to make even basic personnel decisions, let alone decisions about salary and promotions. Michael and his staff won't look at them again until the next year-end dance of performance appraisal. If you could hear Michael's staff talking privately about the process, you would hear comments like "What a joke!" or "This is a waste of time."

Wait, there's more. Michael's department isn't running very well. His staff miss deadlines. They aren't sure who should be doing what, so some things "fall through the cracks," while in other areas they step all over each other getting things done. The same mistakes are made again and again, which drives everybody nuts, but nobody seems to know why they keep happening. Mostly Michael doesn't know what's going on. All he knows is that he is busy and his staff are busy.

Here's the fundamental problem. Michael, his manager, colleagues, and pretty much everyone at Acme see what they call "performance management" as a necessary evil. They do it because they "ought to" or "have to." They don't realize that performance management, if carried out properly, has the potential for fixing many of the problems they're facing.

So, this whole process, with the forms, the superficial meetings, and filing, is a waste. No, it's worse than a waste. Employees think Michael is a poor manager (perhaps they're right) and that affects his credibility. The organization thinks it's accomplishing something, but it's just creating more useless work for people who have better things to do. They're just doing it all wrong. Pure and simple.

Is There Hope?

Yes, there's hope. Acme has a very skilled and dedicated staff. The managers are good folks and bright—even if they need to learn about managing performance. If they knew what performance management means, what it can be used for, and how it can address Acme's business problems, the company could be more success-ful—and the work climate would be better and more enjoyable for everyone.

In fact there's hope for every company and every manager. Does the Acme story sound familiar to

Performance Appraisal Isn't Performance Management

Don't make the mistake of thinking that evaluating or appraising perfor-mance is the same thing as managing performance. It's not. Evaluating per-formance is but one part of a perfor-mance management system. If you only evaluate performance and don't do the other parts, you'll fail.

you? Have you ever done what Michael does? Have you ever had your performance "appraised" in a way that didn't really help you much and maybe even discouraged you from want-ing to improve at all? Probably. Are you getting value from your performance management system? A little? A lot? Probably less than you could get.

Our goal for this book is to explore the basic question, "How can you use performance management as a meaningful tool to help people succeed?" Let's start by looking at what performance management is and what it isn't.

Performance Management: What Is It?

Performance management is an ongoing communication process, undertaken in partnership, between an employee and his or her immediate supervisor that involves establishing clear expectations and understanding about:

- the essential job functions the employee is expected to do
- how the employee's job contributes to the goals of the or-ganization
- what "doing the job well" means in concrete terms
- how employee and supervisor will work together to sus-tain, improve, or build on existing employee performance

- how job performance will be measured
- identifying barriers to performance and removing them

That gives us a starting point and we'll continue to flesh out things as we go. Note some important words here. Managing performance is done with the employee because it benefits the employee, the manager, and the organization, and is best done in a collaborative, cooperative way. Performance management is a means of preventing poor performance, and working together to improve performance. Above all, performance management means ongoing, two-way communication between the performance manager (supervisor or manager) and staff member. It's about talking and listening. It's about both people learning and improving.

Performance management This is an ongoing communication process, undertaken in partnership, between an employee and his or her immediate supervisor that involves establishing clear expectations and understanding about the jobs to be done. It is a system. That is, it has a number of parts, all of which need to be included if the performance management system is going to add value to the organization, managers, and staff.

What Performance Management Isn't

It's important to know what performance management is, but we also need to know what it is not. In our tale about Acme Progressive, Michael thought that performance *appraisal* was the same as performance *management*. Most people at Acme thought performance management was about filling out and filing forms. No surprise that the process had no positive value.

To succeed at performance management, you need to be aware of some common misconceptions that can trip up even the best of managers.

Performance management isn't:
- something a manager does to an employee
- a club to force people to work better or harder

- used only in poor performance situations
- about completing forms once a year

It is an ongoing communication process between two people. That's the key point. If you remember it's about people working with people to make everyone better, you have a much greater chance of succeeding. Everyone wins.

What's the Payoff for Using Performance Management?

As you read more about performance management, you will realize that it takes time and effort—perhaps time and effort you would rather use for other things. What manager wants more work? The reality is that it does take time and effort, but the time and effort are an investment. We need to turn our attention to how that investment brings a return.

When performance management is used properly, there are clear benefits to everyone—managers, employees, and the organization. Let's take a look at those potential benefits.

For Managers

My favorite question to ask managers is, "What things about your job drive you nuts, the things that you take home at the end of the day?" Here are some of their answers:

- feeling the need to micromanage and to be involved in everything to make sure it goes right
- never having enough time in the day
- employees who are too timid to make decisions they could make on their own
- employees' lack of understanding of their jobs, particularly the whys of the jobs
- staff disagreements about who does what and who is responsible for what
- employees giving too little information to managers when information is important
- finding out about problems too late to prevent them from growing

- poor-quality performance
- employees repeating the same mistakes

What common threads can we find in these complaints?

Let's start with micromanaging. One reason why managers feel the need to be involved in everything is they aren't confident their employees are going to do the job the way the manager wants. Wouldn't it make more sense to make sure staff understand what's needed, rather than trying to be involved in everything?

How about not having enough time? When employees don't have a clear idea of what their jobs are, how they should be done, and why, that creates more work for managers. Decisions that employees could make end up on the manager's desk. Little problems that should never involve the manager keep coming up if employees don't understand their jobs well enough to feel they can make good decisions.

What's the common thread? Lack of clarity, lack of shared understanding, and not being on the same wavelength create more work.

What about staff not giving important information to the manager when it's needed? Managers need to know about problems before they get bigger, so they can work to avoid difficulties rather than run around "fighting forest fires." Besides, not having   information can be very embarrassing when your boss asks you how something is going. What's the common thread here? Common understanding of what is important and not important.

Finally, let's turn to poor-quality performance and the repetition of mistakes. If we have no way of helping employees

---

Smart Managing

Identify the Payoffs for Yourself

If you're going to invest the time and effort to do performance management properly, you'll need to know how it's going to pay off. Otherwise you won't be motivated. Periodically remind yourself of why you're doing it and how it's going to save you time and trouble.

learn to be better performers, it's more likely they're going to repeat mistakes and achieve less than they might. If we have no way of diagnosing why mistakes happen, how can we hope to prevent them? We can't—and it's a pretty sure thing that the mistakes are not going to go away on their own.

While performance management cannot solve every problem, it has the potential to address many of these common management concerns. Pay special attention to the word *potential*. If you use it properly, invest the time, and create cooperative relationships, performance management can:

- reduce your need to be involved in everything that goes on (micromanagement)
- save time by helping employees make decisions on their own by ensuring they have the necessary knowledge and understanding to make decisions properly
- reduce time-consuming misunderstandings among staff about who is responsible for what
- reduce the frequency of situations where you don't have the information you need when you need it
- reduce mistakes and errors (and their repetition) by helping you and your staff identify the causes of errors or inefficiencies

To summarize, performance management is an investment up front so that you can just let your employees do their jobs. They'll know what they're expected to do, what decisions they can make on their own, how well they have to do their jobs, and when you need to be involved. This will allow you to attend to tasks that only you can address. That saves time.

For Employees

If performance management is a process done in partnership with staff, we need to address how it benefits staff members. After all, it's hardly realistic to expect employees to participate in a partnership if there are no payoffs for them.

Just as we did for managers, let's look at some common things that drive employees nuts:

- not knowing whether they are doing well or not
- not knowing what level of authority they have
- not getting recognition for a job well done
- not having an opportunity to develop new skills
- finding out the boss has been dissatisfied with an employee's work for a long time
- being unable to make even simple decisions by themselves
- being micromanaged
- not having the resources they need to do their jobs

Performance management can address these concerns. It can provide scheduled forums for discussion of work progress, so employees receive the feedback they need to help assess their accomplishments and to know where they stand. That regular communication ensures there are no surprises at the end of the year. Since performance management helps employees understand what they should be doing and why, it gives them a degree of empowerment—the ability to make day-to-day decisions. Finally, a critical part of the performance management process is figuring out how to improve performance, even if there is no current performance problem. This provides an opportunity to help employees develop new skills and is more likely to identify barriers to better performance, such as inadequate resources.

In summary, employees benefit from better understanding their jobs and their job responsibilities. If they know their limits, they can act more freely within those parameters.

For the Organization

Organizations work more effectively when the goals and objectives of

> **TRICKS OF THE TRADE**
>
> **Explaining the Point to Your Staff**
> Just like managers, staff need to understand the point of performance management and, more specifically, how it's going to benefit them. If they don't understand that, they're unlikely to enter into partnership to make it work. Explain the process and how it will benefit the employees. Ask them how it can be made better so it helps them even more.

the organization, those of the smaller work units, and the job responsibilities of each employee are all linked. When people in the organization understand how their work contributes to the success of the company, morale and productivity usually improve. A company can have all of its parts aimed at the same bull's-eye. Performance management is the key to making these links clear to everyone.

There's another reason why performance management is important. It's a legal reason—and a serious one.

Municipalities, states or provinces, and federal governments have established laws, regulations, and guidelines that apply to what companies can do regarding termination of employment, hiring practices, and discrimination. While laws differ according to jurisdictions, you can count on one thing: there are rules that apply to you. What does that mean to you and your company?

If you have to fire an employee for poor performance, he or she may have legal recourse to challenge that action. The employee could claim the firing was based on some form of discrimination (gender, age, ethnic background) and/or that no warning was given so there was no chance to improve. If a labor grievance is filed or other legal proceedings occur, the company will be expected to provide evidence that the firing was for poor performance. The evidence required to defend the company must be as objective and specific as possible. (In a later chapter we'll map out exactly what that means.)

A properly constructed performance management system includes documenting performance problems in a timely way, tracking how those problems are communicated to the employee, and recording all positive steps taken to remedy the situation. Not only are those records critical in a formal hearing, but the existence of proper records discourages employees from taking frivolous or nuisance-type actions.

Protection from False Allegations

John was an account executive with a public relations firm. While initially John was moderately successful, his sales had declined during the past year. After the first quarter of lower sales, his boss, Dave, met with John, went over the figures, and worked with him to identify possible causes and work out some ideas for improvement. Dave kept records of the meeting and the sales figures.

Unfortunately, despite the meeting and subsequent attempts to resolve the issue, John's sales continued to drop. After trying everything to remedy the situation, Dave decided to let John go. Although John couldn't deny the drop in sales, he felt that his termination was not due to poor performance, but because he belonged to a minority. He threatened to file a complaint with the appropriate government agency.

The parties and their attorneys met and the company provided the detailed documentation of performance problems and Dave's efforts to work with John to solve them. After the meeting, John's attorney advised him that no court would rule in his favor and the complaint was dropped. The evidence compiled through proper performance management prevented a costly legal battle that could have damaged the company's reputation in the eyes of its customers.

Manager's Checklist for Chapter 1

❑ Performance management is an ongoing communication between the manager and each employee to clarify job responsibilities and improve performance continuously.

❑ All parties in a partnership need to know why they are partnering. If you understand the advantages of performance management, you can explain to staff how it will benefit them so they can buy into it.

❑ Don't confuse performance management with performance appraisal. Appraisal is only one part of a performance management system. Managing performance requires that you use all of the components to succeed.

The Challenge of Performance Management

If performance management were easy, every company would be reaping the benefits that come from doing it well. Every manager would look forward to performance planning and appraisal meetings with happy anticipation, and every employee would be jumping at the chance to review his or her performance with the manager. Human resource departments wouldn't have to bug managers to do reviews.

But performance management is a challenge. Managers don't particularly look forward to the process, employees often dread it, and the poor souls in human resource departments spend a good part of their time hounding managers to carry out their performance management responsibilities.

The challenge that you face is to find a way of doing performance management that makes sense to you and your employees, gets you what you need to do your job, helps employees do their jobs, and helps the company achieve its goals. Whether you receive a set of forms and procedures from your company or you're creating your own way to man-

Even the Best Are Challenged

I got a call from a very famous high-tech firm, a company whose products you probably use every day and whose name you would immediately recognize. The company has been highlighted as a leader, an example of great management. But management was struggling with a problem.

Only about half of the managers were turning in their performance management documents. They wanted to know how to get better buy-in and compliance.

My advice? Forget about compliance, forcing people to do them. Instead, build commitment, so employees want to do them because they're useful. Educate managers and employees about how performance management can help them reach their job goals and personal goals.

age performance, you still need to understand what separates a good approach from a poor one. You also need to understand some basic psychology, because, as we've pointed out, performance management is about relationships, communication, and people. If you understand why managers and employees dread traditional performance management, you can come up with solutions to minimize the discomfort and clear the way for a system that is perceived as adding value for everyone. If you understand the basics, the reasons for performance management, what makes a performance management system work, and the human side of the equation, you'll be able to make almost any performance management process work. These are the things we'll discuss in this chapter.

Why Do So Many People Try to Avoid Performance Management?

First things first. Is this an important question? Absolutely. If you don't address the factors that might make you reluctant to undertake performance management, you're much more likely to procrastinate. Many managers end up so skilled at not doing performance management that they never get the process done, despite prodding from those human resource folks. Perhaps more important is understanding why employees may distrust the process or be intimidated by it. If we are to forge partnerships to improve performance, we need to know why people feel discomfort and what we can do about it.

Manager's Reluctance

You're probably the best judge of why you might be uncomfortable using performance management and performance appraisal. But here are a few reasons often cited by managers.

- "The forms and procedures my company makes me use don't make much sense—it's just a whole lot of pointless paperwork."
- "I don't have the time."
- "I hate getting into arguments with employees. No matter what I do, employees feel attacked. It's never pleasant."
- "I have trouble giving feedback to staff or even knowing what they're doing. I can't be watching them all the time."

Forms and procedures that don't make sense. Many companies insist that managers use a set of forms, a particular method, and a schedule that don't fit every situation. Managers may never be consulted about what they would find useful. If you can't see the point of an exercise, it's hard to motivate yourself to carry it out. There are some solutions to the problem, perhaps not perfect solutions but workable.

If you're stuck with forms or an approach you don't like, don't give up. As you'll see later, no performance management system is perfect, ever!

> **Don't Like the Company Approach?** Smart Managing
> Companies tend to want a uniform process to manage performance, which can make the process overly bureaucratic. If you don't find the mandated approach useful to you, develop a way to make it work by focusing on the opportunity to discuss performance with staff, person to person. If you focus on building relationships, involving staff as equals, and communicating, you can make even a bad system work better.

When you focus on performance management as a way of communicating and building relationships, the actual format of the reporting system becomes less important. Work to clarify job expectations with each employee, create a climate of trust and working together, involve employees as partners, and aim your discussions at improving everyone's performance, and you'll succeed—despite the system.

(And if you're in a position of having input into company-wide programs, you might want to involve managers in designing the system.)

No time! Yes, performance management takes time. But, when managers plead "no time to do it," it's often because they misunderstand what performance management can offer. A common misconception about performance management is that it's about "after the fact" discussion and the purpose is to catch mistakes and poor performance after they happen. But that's not the core of performance management. It's not about inspection or looking in the rearview mirror to assign blame. It's about preventing problems and identifying barriers to success before they become costly.

That means that performance management can save management time. When employees don't have clear expectations about what they are to do, when, and how well, they tend to involve managers in issues they could handle themselves. Or they make mistakes because they think they know what to do but don't really know. When staff make inappropriate decisions, they create brush fires (or forest fires) that can require

---

TRICKS OF THE TRADE

The Workplace Oil Change

Managers who use performance management successfully know that the time needed is an investment in preventing problems and saving the time that would be required to solve them if they grew. It's the equivalent to regular oil changes for your car. What's better? Spending a little time and money getting the oil changed or ending up with a dead engine on a highway in the middle of nowhere?

management intervention. And that's where a good deal of management time goes—getting involved in situations unnecessarily and putting out fires.

As the commercial goes, you can pay now or pay a lot more later. Performance management is an investment of time up front to prevent problems and to allow you to use your time to do what you alone can do.

Fear of confrontation. Most people don't like confrontations, conflicts, and arguments. Managers express concern about the difficulty of bringing up performance problems, because they feel that employees are going to fight back, and the process might turn ugly.

Sometimes that happens, but it isn't the norm, and it shouldn't be the norm. Here's why:

- When employees see performance management as a process designed to help rather than to blame, they're much more likely to be cooperative and open.
- Discussions about performance shouldn't be limited to the manager passing judgment on the employee. Employees should be encouraged to evaluate themselves. Manager and employee get to exchange views on performance. Often, employees are actually more critical of their own work than the manager is.
- If managers look at performance management as something they do to employees, confrontation is inevitable. If they view it as a partnership, they reduce confrontation.
- Performance management is not about discussing poor performance. It's about talking about accomplishments, successes, and improvement. A focus on those three things reduces confrontation because manager and employee are on the same side.
- When confrontation occurs or becomes ugly, it's often because managers have avoided dealing with a problem until it's severe. Early identification of problems helps in the resolution process.

So, while it's understandable that managers worry about confrontation, that fear is often a result of looking at performance management as a confrontational approach. Yes, sometimes things can turn unpleasant. But if you set an appropriate climate, use some interpersonal skills we'll talk about later, and not procrastinate, you're more likely to reduce conflict and confrontation.

Feedback and observation problems. Some managers complain they can't give feedback to staff because they don't have time to stand over them and watch them do their jobs every day. It's a good point. You can't stand there watching, because you don't have the time—and because you will drive your employees around the bend. So let each employee be the expert on his or her job and performance.

> **Smart Managing**
>
> ### Reducing Conflict Potential
>
> Smart managers know how to influence the degree of conflict and confrontation. Approach the process as a "We" exercise. Don't give pronouncements on performance, but first engage the employee in self-evaluation. Also, help employees understand how performance management can help them reach their goals.

In some rare situations it may be necessary to observe employees as they work. But for the most part, your role isn't to judge them, but to help them assess their own work as they go. You don't need to watch all the time and you don't need to have all the answers. You and each staff member will work together to find the answers.

Employee's Reluctance

Managers are employees too. You already know some of the reasons why employees might feel uncomfortable with performance management because you've been there too.

As a manager, you're responsible for helping employees feel more at ease with the process. So, what might make an employee feel uncomfortable? Consider the following:

- Many employees have had poor experiences with performance management, perhaps with other managers.
- Nobody likes to be criticized. And employees may have experienced situations where their manager gave them no feedback until their yearly review and then dumped on them. So they're uncomfortable.

> ### Don't Delay
>
> Most managers put off doing performance management because they look at it in the wrong light, as a nuisance. Look at it instead as a problem-prevention technique. Focus on the time you save by preventing problems. If you set a climate of working with staff to do things right, performance and relationships will improve. Then you don't have to procrastinate anymore. And remember: the ultimate goal is to help staff learn to assess their own work, which will save you time.
>
> **Smart Managing**

- When employees don't know what to expect, they become fearful. If so, they may also become aggressive or defensive.
- Employees often don't understand the point of performance management or don't see it as something useful to them.

These are things you can do something about. Later in the book we'll talk about specific techniques to help staff develop positive perceptions of the performance management process. For now, remember that your job includes educating staff so they understand how they can benefit. Remember also that initial discomfort is normal and can be overcome.

Criteria for Performance Management That Works

As a manager, you will make choices about performance management (and there are many) that are going to be the major determinants of how well it works and whether it returns value. Knowing what makes a performance management system work will guide you in making those decisions. We'll help you address some of the important questions, but here are just a very few examples.

- How do I communicate my expectations about employee job responsibilities?
- How do I involve staff as partners?
- How do I broach the subject of poor performance?
- How often do I need to meet with staff?
- How do I make performance management meaningful for everyone?

Our starting point is to state what we mean by an "effective performance management system." An effective system helps organizations, managers, and employees succeed. It helps the organization meet its short- and long-term goals and objectives by helping managers and employees do their jobs better and better. Since performance management is a tool for success, we must look at what organizations, managers, and employees need to succeed. Only then can we understand what an effective performance management system will look like. Let's look at each need separately.

TRICKS OF THE TRADE

A Wonderful Question
Need a good start to open a discussion about performance management with employees? Explain that you need to discuss their jobs to help them get better and better. Ask them, "Since we need to meet on a regular basis, what do you need from me at those meetings to help you do your job better?" Meet those needs and you quickly put everybody on the same performance management team.

Key Term

Effective Performance Management System
A process that helps the organization meet its short- and long-term goals and objectives by helping managers and employees do their jobs better and better.

What Organizations Need to Succeed

There are five factors in organizational success:
1. Organizations need some way to coordinate the work of their units (divisions,

departments, branches) so they are all aimed at achieving the same goals and purposes.

2. Organizations need ways to identify barriers as they arise, catch problems early, and prevent problems. Whether those barriers are individual (staff members who lack needed skills) or related to systems (poorly designed work flow or too much bureaucracy), they need to be identified and addressed as soon as possible.

3. Organizations also need to conform to legal requirements regarding employment, so they're protected.

4. Organizations need a way to gather information to make important human resource decisions. Who should be promoted? Are there special areas where training is needed?

5. Organizations need to be continuously developing their people (both managers and employees) so they can help make the organizations more competitive.

What Managers Need to Succeed

As a manager, no doubt you have a pretty good idea about what helps you do your job well and what you need. But here are a few things to consider.

1. Managers need information about what's going on in their organizations, what's going well, what's going less well, the status of schedules and projects, and so on. You want to get the right amount of information (not too much, not too little) when you need it (not too early, not too late).

2. To help staff improve, managers need information about how well each employee is performing his or her job and how each can improve. If the performance is poor, managers need to know why problems are occurring.

3. Just as with organizations, managers need some way to aim all employees at the same goals and purposes, and to coordinate their efforts in order to achieve those goals.

4. Managers need a way to help employees feel motivated and feel valued. That means having ways of recognizing good performance and of helping everyone succeed.

5. Managers need a way to communicate job expectations

to employees—what's important and less important, and the kinds of decisions employees can make on their own. Why? Because, as you will see, employees need to know those things to succeed.

6. Managers need to have some method of documenting performance problems. There are two reasons for this. First, if managers can't be specific about performance problems, they're not likely to be able to help an employee improve. Second, managers may be expected to justify disciplinary action with precise, specific data about performance difficulties or violation of workplace rules.

What Employees Need to Succeed

Now let's look at what employees need to perform their jobs successfully.

1. Employees need to know what you expect them to do, when, and how well. If they don't know, how can they succeed?

2. Employees need regular, specific feedback on their job performances. They need to know where they are excelling and where they could improve. If they don't know what they should continue to do and what they should change, how can they get better?

3. Employees need to understand how their work fits in with the work of others, the goals of their work unit, and the overall mission and purpose of the company. Why? Because it's motivating to feel part of a larger purpose and to have a sense of helping to achieve that purpose.

4. Employees need to play an active role in defining and redefining their jobs. First, it's motivating to do so. Second, employees, particularly experienced ones, know their jobs better than anyone else and often know best how to remove any barriers to their success.

5. Employees need to know their levels of authority. When they know what decisions they can make on their own, what decisions need to involve others, and what decisions

are managerial, they can operate with greater confidence. This knowledge also speeds up processes.

6. Employees need to have opportunities to develop their skills and grow. An employee who is learning new things and applying them is more likely to stick around and more likely to be motivated.

Our Performance Management Criteria

Now we can link our criteria for an effective performance management approach to what organizations, managers, and employees need to succeed. Performance management should provide:

1. A means of coordinating work so that the goals and objectives of the organization, units, and employees are aimed at the same bull's-eye.
2. A way to identify problems in processes that keep the organization from becoming more effective.
3. A way of documenting performance problems to help the company conform to laws and guidelines (and demonstrate that conformance), to discourage frivolous lawsuits and grievances, and to serve as evidence if necessary.
4. Information for making decisions about promotions, employee development strategies, and training.
5. Information so managers and supervisors can prevent problems, help staff do their jobs, coordinate work, and report to their bosses in a complete, knowledgeable way (so they don't look stupid!).
6. A way for managers to work with employees to identify problem areas, diagnose the causes, and take action to eliminate the problems.
7. A means of coordinating the work of all the employees who report to the same manager.
8. A method of providing regular, ongoing feedback to employees in a way that supports their motivation.
9. A means of preventing mistakes by clarifying expectations, establishing shared understanding of what employ-

ees can and can't do on their own, and showing how each employee's job fits into the big picture.
10. A means of planning employee development and training activities.

Smart Managing

Addressing the Whole Challenge
Think of the performance management process as a system. If you do, you can handle it in a way that meets essential needs while keeping it practical. Focus on the overall purpose. Sometimes trade-offs are necessary. By understanding what performance management is for and how it works, you can make intelligent decisions about the process.

These ten points help aim the performance management system at the goal of improving the organization and everyone's performance. There are a few more points to cover.

We need the performance management system to be practical. If the process is so unwieldy that nobody wants to use it, it's not worth much.

Let's add a few more "practical" criteria for the system:
- It should be as simple as possible.
- It should require the least amount of paperwork and bureaucracy possible.
- It should require the least time investment possible.
- It needs to maximize comfort—or at least minimize discomfort.
- It must serve the needs of managers, employees, and the organization. If managers or employees see it as a waste of time, it isn't going to be very effective.

When Performance Management Approaches Don't Work

Let's end this chapter by talking about what happens when performance management approaches are badly designed, aren't used properly, or are just ineffective.

People may feel that lousy performance management sys-

> ### A Poor System in Action
> Jean struggled with one of her employees, who was often late, missed work, made a lot of mistakes, and treated customers badly. After meeting with the employee several times, Jean finally fired him.
>
> The employee appealed the firing, claiming that it was unfair and not based on any performance failure, because Jean had been using a simple annual report card that rated performance from poor to excellent.
>
> When the case went to court, the company was asked to produce data to justify termination for poor performance, including dates, details, and how each problem had been communicated to the employee. Jean had only a record of absences and a few annual ratings. The company lost the case because the court deemed there was insufficient evidence to prove poor performance.

tems are harmless. That's not true. A poorly implemented approach may be much worse than having none at all. In fact, if you can't or won't do performance management properly, then don't even try. If it isn't helping to increase success, then it's probably causing damage.

What kinds of damage? First, a poor performance management system undermines the credibility of management. When employees consider the system "a waste of time" or "a joke" (which they often do), they also wonder about the intelligence of the managers who would use that system. This situation hurts morale. Systems that are unfair, that are a paper chase without apparent purpose, or that put manager and employee in confrontational positions damage motivation. Good systems solve problems; poor systems create them.

Poor systems also can waste valuable time and other resources on the part of staff, managers, and human resource departments. If you're going to spend time doing it, you need to do it right—unless you've got resources to spare.

Poor systems and execution can provide a false sense of security. The legal system or a labor-management agreement may require certain kinds of documentation when disciplinary action is initiated. Poor systems may not provide the necessary information. Managers may suddenly find themselves caught in a situation in which they're helpless to deal with severe performance problems.

In the next chapter we're going to discuss and evaluate various methods used to manage performance. Before you move on, you might want to take a few moments to answer the following questions:

- Do I know what I want to achieve?
- Am I prepared to invest time up front to save time later?
- Am I willing to work to manage performance in partnership with employees?
- Am I clear about the relationships between the success of the organization, managers, and employees and how a performance management system can help?
- Am I prepared to look at performance management as a major part of my managerial job responsibilities?

Manager's Checklist for Chapter 2

❏ To work, your performance management approach must be useful to the organization, to you, and—perhaps most important—to your employees. The only reason to use performance management is to help everybody be more successful.

❏ Some performance management systems work well. Many do not. We can make them work by being clear about what constitutes a good system and what will allow it to work.

❏ A poor performance management system can be harmful. Decide whether you are willing to do it right (and invest in it) or you are just going through the motions. If you aren't prepared to do it right, it's better not to do it at all.

❏ The challenge of performance management is finding ways to do it that are practical and meaningful. This requires thought and understanding.

3

Performance Management as a System

If you want maximum results from performance management, you need to view it as a system that operates within a larger system. We'll explain what this means in a moment.

First, let's look at why the concept of a "system" is important. We've talked about the consequences of poor performance management systems, the potential for damage, and the time and resources wasted when performance management is done badly. We've also pointed out that one of the major reasons why so many performance management efforts fail is they aren't connected to anything else in the workplace. They aren't connected to job success, performance improvement, employee development, the goals of the organization, or any other important parts of the organization. They just dangle out there. It's no wonder people don't see the point.

The other reason for failure? Managers don't use all the tools of performance management. If you believe that performance *appraisal* is performance *management*, it's just not going to work.

So, we need to understand that performance management is a system and that it must connect to the parts of the larger system—other important functions in your organization.

What Is a System?

We use the word *system* to refer to something that has component parts that interact and work together in an interdependent way to accomplish something.

Take computer *systems,* for example. They consist of parts (monitor, video card, printer, memory, keyboard, and so on) that work together (at least in theory!) to accomplish tasks. The parts are interdependent. If you upgrade the central processing unit (CPU), for example, you won't realize the full benefits unless you have enough memory, because the CPU and the memory interact.

System A set of components that work together in an interdependent way to accomplish something. Systems take inputs and, through a series of processes, transform those inputs into outputs—products, services, or information.

Performance management is a system just like your computer system. Develop or focus on only one part of the system and it won't work. We need to discuss two questions:

- What are the essential parts of an effective performance management system?
- How can we integrate or link a performance management system to the rest of the organization's functions so it is relevant, it has meaning, and it contributes to the overall organization?

The Components of a Performance Management System

Before we describe the different components of performance management, we need to make one critical point. It isn't a linear, straight-line process.

Imagine a staircase. When you climb the stairs, you put your foot on the first stair, then on the next, and so on. Once you've reached the fifth stair, you don't usually jump back down to the first one. That's a straight-line process: you start at step A, go to step B, and then to step C, and so forth.

Performance management isn't like that. In performance management you might start at step A, move to step B, and then back to step A, sometimes having a foot on two steps at the same time. Why? Because it's not a linear process like climbing stairs. It's a dynamic process between two people that changes over time.

> ### Think "Systems"
> The better you link a performance management system to other things the organization must do, the more likely people will understand that it serves an important purpose. Also, you must include all of the parts of a performance management system. Neglect one or two and it isn't going to work.

If this sounds confusing to you, hold on a moment and it will get clearer as we describe each of the components and how they fit together. In later chapters we'll explain how to successfully execute each of the parts of the performance management system. For now we'll keep these descriptions short.

Performance Planning

Performance planning is the usual starting point for an employee and manager to begin the performance management process. Manager and employee work together to identify what the employee should be doing for the period being planned, how well the work should be done, why it needs to be done, when it should be done, and other specifics, such as level of authority and decision making for the employee. Usually performance planning is done for a one-year period, but it can be revisited during that year.

By the end of the performance planning process, both manager and employee should be able to answer the following questions in the same way:

- What are the employee's major responsibilities for the year?
- How will we know whether the employee is succeeding?
- If appropriate, when should the employee carry out those responsibilities (e.g., for specific projects)?
- What level of authority does the employee have with respect to job tasks?
- Which job responsibilities are of most importance and which are of least importance?
- How do the employee's responsibilities contribute to the department or company?
- Why is the employee doing what he or she is doing?
- How can the manager help the employee accomplish the tasks?
- How will the manager and the employee work to overcome any barriers?
- Does the employee need to develop new skills/abilities to accomplish tasks (development planning)>?
- How will the manager and the employee communicate during the year about job tasks, to prevent problems and keep current?

Performance Planning
Starting point for performance management: employee and manager work together to identify, understand, and agree on what the employee is to be doing, how well it needs to be done, why, when, and so on.

While performance planning is mostly about clarifying job tasks for individual employees, it can provide a forum for discussing general issues with all employees. Some managers may want employees to understand that they are expected to refrain from insulting behavior toward their colleagues, to dress appropriately, and so on. Performance planning may include such issues, particularly if they interfere with work.

Process. People vary in how they go about creating a common understanding of the questions listed above. Almost always there will be at least one meeting between the manager and each employee. Sometimes group meetings can be used to make specific project assignments, followed by more detailed, individual meetings. Managers also use different resource materials: some will have employees look at the company's plan for the future before discussing individual roles, while others will start with the formal job description.

Result. What comes out of performance planning besides "common understanding"? Usually the answers to the questions listed previously will be written down in the form of objectives, goals, and standards. This constitutes the employee's plan for the year, which will then be used in the performance appraisal meeting at the end of the period being planned. If employees need development or training to do their jobs, that's also recorded. The format of the plan can vary, but usually this document should be short, clear, and concise—no longer than several pages. Employee and manager both sign the form signifying agreement with its contents.

Ongoing Performance Communication

So, once each employee knows what to do, when, and how well, is that it until performance reviews at the end of the year? *No!*

It's a serious mistake to assume that employees and the organization can run on autopilot. Things change. Projects pop up unexpectedly. Perhaps employee and manager misjudged the time needed to complete a task. Maybe problems occur. We need to treat the *performance planning documents* as dynamic and we need to treat *job performance* as dynamic, so we can remove barriers to performance before they occur or as they occur, *not* months later or at the end of the year. By then too much damage has happened.

Ongoing performance communication is simply a two-way process to track progress, identify barriers to performance, and give both parties the information they need to succeed.

Ongoing performance communication allows manager and employee to work together to prevent problems, deal with any problems that occur, and revise job responsibilities, as is often necessary in most workplaces.

Process. The methods you use to foster that two-way communication will reflect what is needed to promote success in your workplace. Here are some common methods:

- short monthly or weekly status report meetings with each employee
- regular group meetings, in which every employee reports on the status of his or her projects and jobs
- regular short written status reports from each employee
- informal communication (e.g., manager walks around and chats with each employee)
- specific communication when problems crop up, at the discretion of the employee

You can see there's quite a range here in terms of the level of formality, from writing regular reports to just chatting. Is there a best way to do it? No. Clearly, if you have weekly individual meetings and you supervise twenty-five employees, that's all you'd be doing from sunrise to sunset. You have to decide when, how, and how often based on what *both* you and the employee need to succeed. You might even find you need to communicate differently with different staff members. Some may need more involvement on your part and some less. Some jobs require more communication than others.

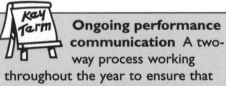

Ongoing performance communication A two-way process working throughout the year to ensure that job tasks stay on track, that problems are red-flagged before they grow, and that both manager and employee keep current.

Use your common sense (and that of the employee) to determine the best way to do it so it's practical and meaningful. Don't set up communication methods that are impossible to carry out.

Result. In some cases, you may not need to produce anything on paper. After all, it's a communication process. In other situations, you may feel that some sort of paper trail is required. Some managers will keep a few notes regarding job status and progress, or keep track of formal regular status meetings. Again, what you record or document depends on your needs. Rather than discuss that here, let's move on to the next component, which we've called "data gathering, observation, and documentation."

Data Gathering, Observation, and Documentation

Whether your concern is helping employees improve, disciplining an unproductive employee, or improving the way work is done, you need data or information to make decisions— and to justify your decisions if necessary. If you want to help an employee improve, you need to know where improvement is needed, where improvement is possible. For legal reasons, if you discipline an employee, you need some proof that he or she isn't performing at an appropriate level. And perhaps most important, if you want to improve the efficiency and productivity of your organization, how do you know where to look and what to change? You need information.

Data gathering is the process of getting information relevant to improvement, whether individual or organizational.

Observation is a way of gathering data. For example, if you walk by the switchboard and hear phones ringing twenty or thirty times, you've *observed* something. That's data. It doesn't tell you what the problem is or how to fix it, but it tells you something could be improved.

Documentation is the process of recording the data gathered so that it's available for use, so it isn't lost. If, when you observe the phones ringing, you write down the time, date, and circumstances, you've documented something.

Let's not make the mistake of thinking that we pay attention to and document only "bad things." We also need to pay attention to the good things, the successes and accomplishments. Imagine that you walk by a customer who is yelling at an employee, and you see that, in a very short time, the employee calms the customer down in a professional and constructive way. You may want to make a mental note of that, or even document it, so you can commend the employee and/or use that information to support a pay raise.

Process. Data gathering, observation, and documentation need to be done according to what's practical and realistic in your workplace. Here are some methods managers use:

- regularly observing by walking around (informal)
- collecting data and information from individual employees at status review meetings
- reviewing work produced by employees
- collecting actual data (e.g., the amount of time it takes to serve each customer, turnaround time, product development, or manufacturing time)
- asking for information (successes/problems) at staff meetings

We need to be careful about this process, so we don't create unintentional and destructive side effects. So let's understand the mind-set.

There are several reasons to gather data and document. The most important, and the one you should focus on, is organizational and individual improvement. To solve problems, you need to identify and understand them. That requires information. The other reason to gather data and document is to protect both the employee and the employer in the event of disagreement. If you need to prove to someone that the phone rang too many times or that a project wasn't completed, then you need data for support, perhaps times and dates.

Unfortunately, these two different purposes can conflict. And which

> **Key Term**
>
> **Data gathering, observation, and documentation** Data gathering is collecting information about the performance of the organization or individuals for the purpose of improving performance. Observation is one means by which a manager can gather data. Documentation is recording the information collected.

one you focus on will determine how you gather data and document. If you focus on protection against lawsuits and take the position your staff isn't trustworthy, you might feel you have to watch them all the time. That's not good. You don't have time for that. Do employees want the boss standing over them all day? No. It creates a bad work climate where productivity and morale suffer. If, however, you begin from the position of trusting staff, you don't have to stand over them and watch. That means staff can gather information and you don't have to rely solely on your own observations. This puts you and staff on the same side. You need to be clear about what you are trying to achieve.

Needless to say, we think the better choice is to trust staff and work with them. Frankly, watching over your staff just isn't practical and isn't a good use of your time. Instead, bring the staff into the data-gathering and improvement process.

Result. What you actually produce depends on what you need. Some people might use special forms to record their observations, while others might scribble them on napkins. You need to determine how much documentation to keep and what form it should take, depending on your answer to the following question: "What records do I need to keep to meet the goals I have set?" Always keep in mind that this isn't a paper chase. If you keep documentation, make sure you know *why* you are keeping it. Don't document just for the sake of doing it. That's a waste of time—unless you're preparing for a career as a private investigator.

> **⚠️ CAUTION!**
> **Avoid Negative Side Effects**
> Unintentional side effects (e.g., anger, lowered productivity, interpersonal problems) occur when we forget *why* we're managing performance and get caught up in following "the book" or "the formula." Always be clear about what you're trying to accomplish. Then, before acting, consider both the positive effects of an action *and* the possible negative side effects. For example, observing staff may provide good information, but it may also send the message that you don't trust their ability or competence.

Performance Appraisal Meetings

Now we've arrived at what most people think is the sum total of performance management, the performance appraisal process. We'll repeat the point once more: if *all* you do is appraisal, if you don't do planning and have ongoing communication, collect data, and diagnose problems, you're wasting your time.

The performance appraisal process involves manager and employee working together to assess the progress that the employee has made toward the goals set in performance planning, and to summarize what has gone well during the period under review and what has gone less well.

But it can be much more than that. It's a communication process, a forum for discussion that doesn't have to focus only on the individual employee. You can use the forum to uncover processes and procedures in the company that are inefficient, unproductive, or destructive. So the review meeting should *not* be only about evaluating the employee. It's an opportunity to solve problems.

The performance appraisal process provides:
- feedback to employee that's formal, regular, and recorded
- documentation for a personnel file that may be used for determining promotions, pay levels, bonuses, disciplinary actions, etc.
- an opportunity to identify how performance can be improved, regardless of current level
- an opportunity to recognize strengths and successes
- a springboard for planning performance for the next year
- information about how employees might continue to develop
- an opportunity for a manager to identify additional ways to help employees in the future
- an opportunity to identify processes and procedures that are ineffective and costly

Process. There are a number of ways to do performance appraisal meetings. In a later chapter we'll walk you through the process and principles, but for now we'll give you a brief overview.

First, prior to the meeting some preparation is done. That might include the manager and employee doing independent appraisals on their own, reviewing objectives and standards, compiling questions, and so on. The preparation should shorten the time needed in the meeting and help both the manager and the employee refresh their memories.

During the meeting, the manager and employee work together to come to agreement on the employee's performance during the past year. They try to stick to specifics and use data rather than vague recollections. Where problems have occurred, the focus isn't on blaming, but on identifying the cause of the problem and formulating a strategy (see "Performance Diagnosis and Coaching" section later in this chapter) to prevent the problem from recurring. Another common and useful process is to plan development activities or training for the employee. Would the employee benefit from some training in a new area? Perhaps he or she might benefit from some job experience in another position? These are useful questions to examine.

Some managers combine a performance appraisal meeting with performance planning, so the performance management cycle is complete. So, in that situation, you review the past year's performance, and then set objectives and standards for the upcoming year. (Warning: this may result in very long, tiring meetings.)

> **Performance appraisal meeting** A process where manager and employee work together to assess the degree to which the employee has attained agreed-upon goals, and work together to overcome any difficulties encountered. Also called "performance review meeting" or "performance evaluation meeting." Usually refers to an annual meeting.
>
> *Key Term*

Results. The discussions in the performance appraisal meeting need to be documented. There are a number of ways to do that, depending on what the company demands and what is useful to manager and employee. For example, some companies require that some sort of rating form be used to summarize the performance appraisal discussions. Others may have more flexible forms or provide leeway regarding what the manager must send on to the personnel office. In any event, there *must* be documentation. Generally, that documentation is signed by both parties. In some cases, where manager and employee disagree with what is written down, the employee may add comments to indicate his or her disagreement.

Finally, if the manager is combining performance planning with performance appraisal, the plan (including goals, objectives, job tasks) will also be produced.

Performance Diagnosis and Coaching

At the beginning of this chapter, we talked about performance management as a nonlinear process, one that involves jumping around from part to part. Performance diagnosis and coaching are very important parts of a performance management system. However, they're not things you do just once or every so often. They permeate or touch every other part of the performance management system. They're the problem-solving component of performance management.

When some sort of problem is identified—whether it's an employee not achieving what was agreed upon or a department falling short—it's critical to determine *why* that problem occurred. Without diagnosing the root cause of the problem, how can we prevent it from happening again? We can't.

For example, if certain employees don't meet several of their objectives, there could be various causes for that performance deficit. Do they lack the skills needed? Didn't they work hard enough? Are they poorly organized? Or maybe the

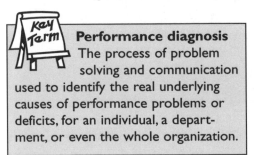

Performance diagnosis The process of problem solving and communication used to identify the real underlying causes of performance problems or deficits, for an individual, a department, or even the whole organization.

cause has little or nothing to do with the employees. Did other people in the organization withhold needed resources? Were the raw materials needed not available? Was the manager unclear about what needed to be done? So, problem diagnosis is vital—and it should be a continuous part of the performance management process.

Once the cause of a performance deficit is identified, manager and employee (and perhaps others in the organization) need to work together to remove the barriers and prevent the deficit. When a manager plays the role of mentor, teacher, or helper, we usually call that "coaching." The manager works with the employee to help him or her develop knowledge and skills in order to improve performance.

Why is this important? Too often managers judge or assess an employee, conclude that he or she has fallen short on some aspect of the job, communicate that to the employee, and then leave it to him or her to figure out how to fix the problem. Some managers take the position that it's solely the employee's responsibility to improve. It may be an interesting philosophical point, but it isn't very practical.

> **Coaching** A process in which a person who is more knowledgeable on a particular issue works with an employee to help him or her develop knowledge and skills in order to improve performance.

Most employees want to improve. Sometimes they need a bit of help. Smart managers know that a small investment in occasional coaching can benefit everyone. Since an employee who improves helps the manager, the department, the organization, and even co-workers, it makes sense to consider improvement as a shared responsibility.

Process. There are as many ways of diagnosing performance and coaching as there are people. We'll talk about them in detail in a later chapter. *The key point:* problem diagnosis and coaching occur throughout the year. They can be used as part of the appraisal process, but they also fit in whenever managers and employees communicate about performance (e.g., regular meetings during the year, staff meetings).

Result. Apart from producing solutions to prevent problems, the diagnostic process and the coaching process may be documented for future reference, if there's a good reason to do so. For example, it may be a good idea to keep track of coaching sessions to document the efforts a manager makes to improve a particular staff member's performance. Or, in diagnosing problems, you might generate work flowcharts or basic notes that might be useful in the future. In other cases, the diagnostic process could result in a written improvement action plan—a brief description of the problem and steps that need to be taken (when, by whom, how) to address it.

Back to Square One—Planning Again

After you do the annual performance review, coupled with the other parts of the system, you begin anew. Armed with the results from the discussion of last year's work, what went well and not so well, and why, you now incorporate that knowledge into the planning process for the next year.

Where Performance Management Fits into the Big Picture

You and your organization make an investment in performance management. To get the best possible return, performance management needs to link up to other processes in the organization. Performance management takes information from other processes and sends information to those other processes. What other processes? Let's look.

Strategic Planning and Company Direction

Many companies have some means of looking to the future. Strategic planning at the corporate level can include a description of the general mission of the company, its values, and, perhaps most important, its goals for the long term. That plan can then be translated into year-by-year plans that align with the longer-term strategic plan.

Where is the link to performance management? Both long- and short-term goals must be translated into goals and objectives for each smaller work unit and then into goals and objectives for each employee. That "translation" from company goals to individual responsibilities is done through the performance planning process we outlined earlier in the chapter. That process aligns the work of each employee with company purpose.

Beyond the alignment of purpose, the information collected from performance management can be used in the planning process. When you are planning, it's great to identify any barriers to success. Performance diagnosis provides valuable information about possible barriers. The more information we have about potential problems, the better we can prepare to avoid or overcome them.

Pay Levels, Rewards, and Promotions

Companies need to make decisions regarding pay levels, bonuses and other rewards, and promotions. An effective performance management system is helpful in making those decisions. If you don't base them on performance, you're likely to be undermining your success.

Human Resource Development Planning

"Human resource development planning" is the fancy term for "helping employees improve." In a constantly changing workplace, the skills needed for employee success change over time. Many companies take a proactive approach to help staff develop new skills by using performance management systems to identify gaps between what employees can do now and what they need to be able to do. Based on that information, which can be generated as part of the performance management process, companies can arrange for training, coaching, job shares and exchanges, formal education, and so on.

Be Sure You Know

Understand how managing performance fits in with other processes in *your* workplace. How can it be better integrated? How should performance management be influenced by budgets, planning, hiring? How should the results of performance management affect those other processes? Performance management takes input from other processes and informs or outputs to other processes.

Budget Processes

Budgeting is a core process in any company. Performance management is linked to it in two ways. First, the budget for an organization may limit what employees can and can't do in carrying out their duties. Performance management is an ideal forum to ensure that all employees understand these constraints. So, budgets provide input into performance management.

Performance management discussions can also provide information to assist in the budgeting process. For example, in performance planning, a manager and an employee identify a technological barrier to successful completion of a project. By identifying this in advance, they can budget additional funds to purchase new equipment so the project can be completed.

Manager's Checklist for Chapter 3

❏ Performance management is a system within a larger system. To get maximum benefit, you need to do the whole process, not just a part of it.

❏ Performance management links up with strategic planning, budgeting, employee development, employee compensation systems, and quality improvement programs. The more links established between performance management and other processes in the organization, the better the return on investment.

Getting Ready: Preparing to Start the Process

OK. You want to start a new way of doing performance management, a way that focuses on communication, tying performance management to other things going on in the organization, and you want to do it efficiently and effectively. Where do you begin?

Let's discuss two starting points. The first is gathering the information you need to create meaningful, measurable goals with each staff member. The second is laying the groundwork so you can work with employees throughout the process.

Getting Your Information and Data

Since part of the power of performance management comes from helping the organization, its units, and all of its employees "pull in the same direction," the more information you and employees have about where the organization is going and how it's going to get there, the better you'll be able to link individual performance expectations to the success of the organization. It's also good for the employees, because they need to know how their jobs and tasks contribute to the overall effort. This provides much more meaning and motivation.

What kinds of information and documents will be helpful? Let's look at a list for the "big picture." The following may be useful in forging the links between *employee* purpose and *organization* purpose:

- the strategic plan of the company
- the one-year (short-term) operational plan of the company
- strategic and operational plans for the next-smallest subunit (e.g., division or department)
- strategic and operational plan for your own work unit
  For the "smaller picture," you may also need:
- job descriptions for each employee
- the performance appraisal information for each employee for the previous year

Let's go through these items to explain why it will help you to have the information and how you will use it in the first step of performance management: performance planning.

Strategic and Operational Plans

Since we suggest that you get these plans prior to embarking on performance management, we should explain what they are. That's difficult, at least for strategic plans, since there are probably as many definitions of that term as there are companies.

Generally, a strategic plan is a document that sets out where the company is going over a certain period of years. It may explain the business of the company, its values and principles, and the goals it has set for the period. It may also include an analysis of the external factors that might affect the business (economy, demographics, etc.), a

Smart Managing

More Information Is Better
The more "big picture" information you have, the better you will be able to align individual job tasks with the needs of your unit and company. Some information might not be available when you need it. In that case you have to make the best of the situation, but it shouldn't stop you from continuing.

look at past performance to determine future targets, and an identification of the resources the company needs to achieve its long-term goals.

Strategic plans aren't just for the company as a whole. The planning should cascade down—although that doesn't often happen. First, the top

> **Strategic Plan** A document mapping out the longer-term strategy, goals, and vision for the company or for each work unit.

managers go through the strategic planning process for the company. The plan that results provides an umbrella under which the smaller divisions or departments do their strategic planning. Then, the strategic plan devised for each division or department provides an umbrella for the component units in their planning process.

This cascading of strategic planning is very logical. Why? Because the purpose, roles, goals, and values of each unit should support or link up with the company's purpose, roles, goals, and values. Then, if each unit achieves its strategic objectives, the company will have achieved its strategic objectives as well, because the objectives are linked.

Operational plans are a bit different from strategic plans. They deal with a shorter time span, often just one year. They may also be much more detailed and more focused on exactly what each work unit must accomplish in any given year. Like strategic plans, operational plans can exist for the company as a whole, the larger subunits, and on down to the smallest work units. In theory, each yearly operational plan needs to be consistent and take into account the larger strategic plans.

OK. So now you've got strategic plans and operational plans. But why do you need them before you start the individual performance planning process? Because the tasks and objectives of each employee are going to be determined, to some degree, by the larger goals. It's that simple, at least in theory. Let's look at a concrete example.

The Argon Company consists of three divisions: human resources, production, and sales. Within each of those divi-

Operational Plan
Usually based on and consistent with the strategic plan (a more detailed plan), with very specific objectives and covering a shorter period of time (perhaps only one year).

sions there are several smaller units. In its strategic planning process, Argon executives addressed the concern that new competitors might take a significant market share from Argon unless they took action over the next five years. They identified two strategic goals or objectives they felt were vital to stay in business:

- maintain or increase current market share over the next five years
- increase profitability by reducing waste

Based on these two strategic goals, the company, in its yearly operational plan, set two specific goals:

- maintain or increase current market share this year by identifying and contacting new clients
- reduce waste and faulty products by 5% this year

Then, the three divisions were expected to identify how they would contribute to these goals over the long term and the short term. They came up with some strategies for doing so. For example, the Human Resources Division created the following strategic objectives for the five-year period:

- provide ongoing training in identifying causes of poor quality
- establish a reward system to encourage employees to identify potential clients

...and the following operational objectives for the current year:

- determine needs for training and development in discovering the causes of poor quality
- identify ways to deliver training in a cost-effective way
- examine hiring practices to determine whether more effective sales staff can be hired and retained

The Production Division and the Sales Division each established different objectives, of course, but also aligned with the corporate plans.

The process continued in a similar way with the smaller units. For example, within the Human Resources Division, the training branch took on the objectives involving training, while the personnel branch took on the objectives related to hiring, retaining, and rewarding.

Finally, in the performance management planning meetings, each branch manager set with his or her employees the goals and objectives for each employee so they reflected the objectives of the branch. For example, the training branch manager assigned one employee to identify training needs and another to find cost-effective ways to deliver that training. In a later chapter we'll discuss how these individual goals are used to review performance at the end of the year.

So, at Argon, each employee contributes to the goals of his or her branch, each branch contributes to the goals of the division, and each division does its share toward achieving the company goals. That's what we mean by integrating performance management into the big picture. And that's why you need information about strategic and operational plans. This helps to form the basis for your performance management, in the planning process described in the next chapter.

> **Involve Staff in Planning**
>
> **TRICKS OF THE TRADE**
>
> Regardless of what the rest of the company does, many managers find it useful to set aside one day a year to meet with staff and identify what the unit needs to accomplish in the coming year. This ensures that staff are on the same page, it's generally motivating and empowering, and it reduces the amount of "paper plans imposed from above." This approach works particularly well when there are no more than twenty people in the unit.

If Information Is Missing and Reality Intervenes

If you're thinking that the above process sounds like quite an undertaking, you're correct. The truth is that many of the managers in many companies don't really know what they're trying to achieve or where they're going. They don't plan very

Smaller Businesses

Although we've used a large company as an example, the cascade approach to planning applies to any business. You need to be flexible. If you manage a restaurant with a staff of seven, for example, you can still follow the same pattern, although you won't have so many documents to examine—if any. So long as you know what the restaurant needs to do to succeed, short term and long term, you can link individual job roles to hitting those targets.

well, so when they hit the mark it's often by accident. Or, they don't plan in a timely way to support performance management with employees.

If you work in one of these organizations, you may not be able to collect the information we've outlined because it doesn't exist. What then?

Let's imagine your company doesn't really have a plan, either long or short term. Let's also assume your division doesn't either. You may not be able to make your bosses come up with strategic and operational company and division plans, but you can still plan for your own unit.

If you've been working for the company for a while, you probably have some idea of what it needs to do to succeed. You should be able to use that informal knowledge to determine what your unit needs to do over the next several years or during the one coming up. So, even if your superiors don't do things perfectly, you can still link individual performance objectives to the objectives you develop for your unit. At the least, you should establish clear links between each employee's objectives and job tasks and the objectives and purpose of your unit. The bare minimum? You need to know where your work unit is going to be able to figure out what employees need to be doing to get it there!

Some "Smaller Picture" Information

Apart from the "big picture" information we've described, you'll find two other things useful, if not essential.

First, you'll want to have job descriptions for every employee—if they exist. What's a job description? It's a statement that usually describes the responsibilities, job tasks, and levels of authority for a position. Often a job description is developed for hiring, to tell potential applicants about the job. It may also be used to determine pay levels.

How is the job description useful in performance management and planning performance? It can be a good starting point if it's done well, since it will outline job tasks and responsibilities. If you've got good job descriptions, use the lists of responsibilities to generate specific objectives and expectations about what constitutes good performance for each job.

Don't Wait Forever
You can never get the performance management process perfect. But since it's a people process, it doesn't have to be perfect. If information is missing, try to obtain it or at least to fill in any critical blanks. But don't wait for other parts of the organization to do it for you—or you may wait forever.

There's a problem, though. While many experts suggest using job descriptions as a guide in setting objectives, many job descriptions are horribly out-of-date. It's costly and time-consuming for companies to update their job descriptions. Unfortunately, the reality is that work changes so quickly that job descriptions can become outdated in a single year, as responsibilities change. Employees often end up doing things not in their job descriptions. So, if you use a job description as a starting point, review and modify it—early on in the performance planning process—so it really reflects what the employee does. We'll talk about that in the next chapter.

The second piece of "smaller picture" information you'll need is a copy of the employee's last formal performance review and any related documentation that might be relevant. Since the performance review and the performance planning meeting are

Antiques Alert!
Many job descriptions are outdated. Don't rely on what you read. Verify with the employee that the job description accurately reflects what he or she really does *now*.

often combined or take place around the same time, this won't be an issue.

Why do you need this information? Because if there were any problems during the last year, you want to take action with the employee to address them.

So, assuming that you've gathered the information we've described, or as much of it as possible, what else do you need to prepare for your performance planning meetings?

Preparing and Educating Staff

By the time you begin the performance management cycle (and after you finish this book), you'll know about the purposes and process of performance management. We've stressed often that performance management is a *people* process and a *partnership* with employees. What's left? Employees need to understand what performance management is for, how it's going to work, what to expect, and what will be expected of them. This is absolutely critical.

If employees don't understand the process and how it will benefit them, they'll worry about it. They'll see it as something done to them and probably focus on the appraisal or evaluation part. The more questions and concerns they have about the process, the more likely they'll enter into it with resistance, hostility, or anger. That puts you behind the eight ball when you're developing a cooperative climate for the process.

As a manager, you must prepare and educate your staff. You can get help from the human resources department, but the bottom line is that your staff need to know what *you* are going to do with them, and that can vary from manager to manager. They need to hear it from you.

How to Prepare and Educate Staff

First, let's outline what staff need to know in order to work with you in the performance management process. They need to know:

• why performance management is important (purpose)

- how will it benefit them, you the manager, and the company
- your general philosophy or approach (e.g., working together, centered on self-evaluation, focus on prevention of performance problems)

They need to know what to expect at the initial meeting:

- What will happen during performance planning meetings?
- What kinds of input are they expected to supply?
- What kinds of questions will you be asking them?
- How will decisions be made during the meetings?
- How flexible will the objectives and job tasks be?
- What kinds of preparation do they need to do?
- How long will the meetings take?

They'll also want to know details about the later parts of the process, particularly about the appraisal meeting:

- What will happen at the yearly review?
- How will disagreements be handled?
- How will the appraisals affect pay, bonuses, and so on?

Employees are sure to have a lot of questions and concerns. What's the best way to help them understand what's happening? Probably the most efficient way is to hold a general staff meeting to explain the process. It should precede your performance planning meeting by a few weeks. You should do this every year, to explain the process to new hires, remind experienced employees, and keep everyone focused on what's important.

Let's bring this chapter to a close by looking at how one manager prepared staff before beginning individual meetings with them. This is just one good way to handle the matter, based on the

CAUTION!

Employee Negativity

Understand that many employees have had bad experiences with performance management and may react negatively to a new or unfamiliar system, even if that system will ultimately help them. Explain it as well as you can, but accept that some will be resistant. Even the best explanation is just words; negative employees will need proof in action. When they see you act in cooperative ways to help them, then they will believe.

specific circumstances of the situation. Note the tone, the style, and the details.

What Staff Preparation Looks Like

George is the director of a work unit of eighteen people. Because of a flattening of the organization, all staff report directly to him (no supervisors). He's introducing a new performance management method. He's called a staff meeting to discuss the new way of doing things. This is what he says:

> Over the last year we've changed a lot around here. Some of you have commented that you aren't getting enough guidance about your work and that sometimes you really don't know what's important to do and what's less important. You've also commented on the rating system we've been using to evaluate performance, saying that it hasn't been helpful. The company has decided to change how we do some things. I think the changes will benefit all of us, including me. We're all going to have a better idea of where we are going and what we need to do. This will also help us catch problems as they occur during the year.
>
> We'll start our new performance management system in about two weeks. I'll set up meetings with each of you so we can discuss what's important about your job, how it fits with our bigger goals, and where and how you should be focusing your energies. We'll agree on some targets, which we'll then use at the end of the year to evaluate the progress made by our unit and by each of you.
>
> After we've set those objectives in our initial performance planning meetings, we'll also set up ways of communicating with each other so that I know what's going on with each of you throughout the year and can help you achieve your goals. After all, that's my job—to help you get your work done.

Smart Managing	**Communicate and Communicate Again**

It's easy for people to misunderstand or forget. It's always a good idea to provide a written summary of key points. Keep it short.

Since our first step is the meetings beginning in a few weeks, let's talk about what we'll be doing.

George explains the relationships among the company's goals, the branch's goals, and each person's individual goals.

In the meetings we're going to determine if your job description is accurate.

Sell the New Way

When introducing a performance management system, stress the benefits for everyone, including employees. There are many, including clearer understanding of priorities, more decision-making power, less need to consult the manager, knowing where you stand throughout the year, no surprises.

Managers commonly make the mistake of focusing on why the system is good for the *company*. Staff need to know how it will be good for *them*.

We want to know how you can best contribute to the goals of the organization. Together, we'll set some targets for you. I'm going to ask you a lot of questions, because each of you is the expert at your job. Here are some things I'll ask:

- Is your job description accurate? What needs to be updated?
- How do you see yourself best contributing to the goals of our work unit?
- What's the best way of measuring your contributions at the end of the year?
- How can I help you hit your targets/goals? What do you need from me?
- What barriers do you see as affecting your job performance? How can we overcome them?
- What authority levels do you need to do your job?
- What are the most important parts of your job?

I'd like you to think about these questions before we meet. That will save us a lot of time. You might want to jot some notes down between now and when we meet.

At the end of our meeting, both of us should know what you need to be doing next year and how we'll be reviewing your performance at the end of the year. We'll put some of this stuff on paper so we can refresh our memories throughout the year.

That's where we are going to start. Let me explain how we will use that information throughout the year and at the end of the year, and how this is going to help all of us.

George provides more information, then concludes:

To summarize, I'll be setting individual meetings with you, about an hour apiece. Between now and the meeting, I'd like you to review your job descriptions, review the objectives our unit is expected to reach this year, and read the short version of our overall company plan. Also think about the questions I'm going to ask you and perhaps make some notes.

Now I know this is new to all of us and we'll be feeling around a bit. You probably have a lot of questions. You can ask them now or, if you prefer, you can pop in over the next few days if you have any concerns.

George opens the floor for questions.

Manager's Checklist for Chapter 4

❑ Preparing for the performance planning meeting is critical to paving the way for a more comfortable process where parties will feel at ease.

❑ Identify any documentation or material you will need at the meetings. Make sure employees have what they need beforehand (e.g., job descriptions, last year's performance review) and have a chance to review it.

❑ If you're doing things a new way, communicate, communicate, and communicate. Explain the details, explain the benefits, and explain the point. Provide a written summary of the process. The more employees understand, the easier the process will be, the more you'll be able to work *with* staff, and the less anxiety will be created.

❑ To save time, staff can do some premeeting work to address the questions you'll be asking them. Explain why this prework is important and how it will save time.

Performance Planning

Too many people believe that *appraisal* is the most important part of performance management. *Planning* is by far much more important.

Why? Because appraisal just looks in the rearview mirror. Planning looks to the future to maximize performance to come, not to analyze performance that is past and unchangeable. The real increases in productivity come from aiming the employee at the bull's-eye, and then getting out of the way.

Let's define performance planning. It's a process in which employee and manager work together to determine what the employee should be doing in the next year and what successful performance means.

Other important parts of performance planning discussions are:

- identifying assistance the manager will provide
- identifying barriers to achievement and means to overcome them
- developing a shared understanding of the relative importance of job tasks (priorities) and levels of authority

Some Issues

In this chapter, we'll address two issues: the people side of performance planning and a few nuts and bolts of the process for setting objectives and standards. Before we do that, we have to consider a few things.

> **Key Term**
>
> **Performance planning**
> The process in which the employee and manager work together to plan what the employee should do in the upcoming year, define how performance should be measured, identify and plan to overcome barriers, and come to a common understanding about the job.

We're going to use a modified version of what some call "management by objectives (MBO)" or sometimes "management by results." The process we discuss is the best way, although not perfect, to deal with performance in a systematic and organized way. While many books on MBO or management by results stress the importance of technical skills involved in performance planning, we aren't going to do that. If you need to know all about goals, objectives, results, key result areas, standards of performance, engineered standards, objective standards, subjective standards, and so on, there are other resources available.

Here's why we're not going to give you a dozen new definitions. The simple purpose of performance planning is to create common understanding between manager and employee. If you achieve that, it doesn't matter whether you know all the terms or variations. If you want to learn the definitions, that's fine, but you don't need them to succeed at performance management or performance planning. Many managers feel defeated and overwhelmed by all the terms and technical stuff. We're going to make it as simple and as practical as possible and not get caught up in definitions or semantics.

We also need to talk about perfection—about writing "perfect" objectives or standards. Too many managers waste time trying to get them perfect, to make them perfectly measurable or perfectly objective (no subjectivity allowed). This attempt at perfection discourages people from carrying out the process.

Keep the following in mind. It's crucial. The less important the job task, the easier it will be to measure it exactly and objectively. The more important the job task (and the more complex), the more difficult it will be to measure it. For example, you can measure the number of rings it takes for an employee to answer phone calls. That's easy. How do you measure the quality of service the employee offers while on the phone? It's much more difficult to do that, because the task is more complex— and more important. So, let's put aside the myth that it's possible to measure everything in an exact and meaningful way.

Avoid the Search for Perfection

Smart Managing

You and your employee can't write perfect objectives and standards. If you try to be "technically correct," you run the risk of making the process horribly frustrating and difficult. Perfection paralysis can be an insidious disease. Focus on creating common understanding. Save the search for perfection for management consultants and researchers.

An Overview of the Performance Planning Process

Performance planning involves face-to-face meetings and some work done by the manager and employee separately. We're going to outline the overall process, paying special attention to the face-to-face part of the process, the performance planning meeting(s). That's where the people process lives.

Purpose and Outcomes

The purpose of the performance planning process can best be defined in terms of the outcomes. By the conclusion of the performance planning process:

- The job tasks and objectives of the employee will be aligned with the goals and objectives of the work unit and the company. The employee will understand the link between his or her responsibilities and the overall goals.

- Job descriptions and job responsibilities will be modified to reflect any changes in the work context.
- Manager and employee will agree on the major job tasks for the employee, how success will be measured, what job tasks are most important and least important, and the level of authority the employee has with respect to each job responsibility.
- Manager and employee will identify any help the manager can provide, any potential barriers to achieving the objectives, and means of overcoming the barriers.
- A formal document (a performance plan) will be produced that summarizes the discussions and agreements and is signed by both manager and employee.

The Process/Steps

We can divide performance planning into three major phases: preparing, meeting, and finalizing the process.

First, preparing. We've talked about linking performance management to other processes in the organization. To do that, both manager and employee have to be familiar with where the organization is going. That's something that can be done before they meet. Also, the employee can review the job description independently. So, the preparation phase may involve manager, employee, or both in reviewing:

- the company's strategic or operational plans (or goals)
- the work unit's plans or goals and objectives
- the last performance appraisal and/or performance plan
- the employee's current job description

The second phase, the heart of performance planning, is the meeting. That's when manager and employee sit down, usually in private, to discuss work for the next year. We'll walk you through the process shortly, but here are the principles we'll apply.

- Since the employee is usually the most familiar with his or her job, the planning process involves a relatively equal partnership between manager and employee. They are negotiating together, because they share a common interest—success.

- Because the employee is an expert in the job, it is the employee who should, by and large, be generating the criteria used to gauge success, with the manager's involvement.
- The manager may be more expert in the "big picture" issues and how the employee fits with other employees and the needs of the work unit and organization. That's a major contribution on the manager's part.
- Because the manager initiates performance planning, it's the manager's job to create a climate for real dialogue and teamwork during the meeting.

Finally, there may be a final phase or review phase where manager and employee tie up any loose ends or sign off on objectives and standards. This could be in the form of a shorter, follow-up meeting.

The Performance Planning Meeting

We're going to create a "road map" for the performance management meeting. As you go through it, keep in mind you can modify it to suit your needs and the needs of employees. Since we're focusing on the people side, we'll provide examples of dialogue for each of the parts of the meeting.

Let's introduce you to the two people involved in our examples. Neil is a management consultant and instructional designer in a somewhat flexible, dynamic work environment that changes a good deal. Sharlene is Neil's manager. Neil and Sharlene are meeting for performance planning about two weeks after they reviewed Neil's performance for last year and about a month after all the staff met to discuss goals and objectives for the entire work unit.

Climate Setting and Focusing

In setting the climate and the focus, we want to get comfortable and focus on our reasons for meeting and what the outcomes should be. Generally the manager is responsible for kicking off the process. How does Sharlene do it with Neil?

Before Neil arrived, Sharlene arranged for coffee to be available in the office and made sure she had copies of Neil's job description, his last performance review, and some information about the work unit's objectives for the upcoming year. She placed a high priority on the meeting, so only a dire emergency could cause its cancellation, and she made sure that nobody would interrupt the meeting.

Avoid Sending the Wrong Message

One mistake managers make is to treat the performance planning meeting as something that can be moved around, interrupted, or canceled. That sends a horrible message, that the process isn't very important. If you think it's important enough to do, then do it right. Keep the appointment and respect it: no cancellations, no interruptions. Employees will take it seriously if you do.

When Neil arrived, she offered him a cup of coffee and they chatted for a minute or two. Then Sharlene moved to focusing the meeting.

She said: "Neil, this is the third year you and I have done this, so I imagine I don't need to give you a long explanation of what we are going to do. But let me do a quick review. Our task is to come to some common understanding about your job responsibilities, what you should be doing, and how we can measure success. But this is also a chance to talk about what I can do to help you and a chance for you to clarify anything you want to talk about with respect to the job or our work unit. Before we get started, are there any issues or questions you feel we need to talk about?"

Focus Fast, and Then Interact

It's important to involve the employee early in the meeting. If you give a detailed explanation of the planning meeting to all staff earlier in the week, all you need to begin each meeting is a few words to set the focus. Then start the interaction.

Neil replied: "Something's been bugging me about team-work and I really would like to talk about it today. Now that we're all moving to a team environment, I've got some questions about what that's going to mean to me as man-agement consultant and instructional designer. I'm not sure how I could contribute to our team here or what you expect from me in that respect. I'd really like to talk about that."

> **Maximizing Meeting Time**
> Make the most of your meeting time by focusing on the communication part, the people part of the meeting. The better prepared you are, the more you can focus on communication and shared understanding.
>
> *Smart Managing*

Sharlene made a note, then said: "Good question. Let's come back to that. You know, maybe that's something I should discuss with all the staff. I really hadn't thought of that."

Reviewing Relevant Information

Before manager and employee can talk about specific job re-sponsibilities, they need to be sure both understand what the work unit needs, where it is going, and any other information that provides a context and meaning for their discussion of specific job responsibilities.

This is how Sharlene started the process. "Well, Neil, you were at our branch planning meeting, so you know what we need to do to help the company meet its goals. You recall we talked about contributing to reducing plant accidents, helping to lower sick leave..."

Sharlene continued summarizing the main points. Then she asked, "Given these targets, where do you see yourself fit-ting into the work unit plan?"

Neil jumped in: "Well, I know the data we reviewed at the branch planning meeting suggested we might need to beef up our workplace health and safety training, but we aren't sure what that would look like. As instructional designer, I guess the job of determining what we need rests with me, as should

Smart Managing

Ask, Don't Tell

Sharlene does a very interesting thing here. She asks Neil where he thinks he can contribute, rather than telling him. Why? Because she wants to take into account his preferences, if possible, since she knows he'll suggest tasks he wants to do. If he's off base, she could guide and negotiate.

the design of any programs we decide on. There are other areas where I might fit, for example, in the areas of stress management consulting and training, and safety audits, since I have some experience in those areas."

Sharlene replied, "That's good. That's pretty close to my thinking. But I want to make sure that you don't get overloaded. The company has set some timelines that are pretty brutal. But that's a good start. We'll come back to that, but I have a few more questions to ask about your job description."

Sharlene pulled out a copy of Neil's job description. "The Personnel Office has asked us to review job descriptions. That's a good idea every year. Here are your major responsibilities and the amount of time you're expected to spend on course design, consulting, and so on. Given what you already know, and taking into account what you did last year, do these figures make sense? Or do we need to adjust them?"

Neil mentioned that he thought the time he spent on course design had increased, from 20% to 50%. He suggested modifying the job description to reflect that increase and the current needs of the unit. After a brief discussion, both agreed.

Sharlene decided to summarize. "OK, so we've agreed you can best contribute over the next year or two by bumping up your course design time to about half of your time. That certainly reflects our needs. And, I think we agree that your role is critical in the areas of accident prevention, identifying how we might go about that, and perhaps additional course design. Are we on the same wavelength so far?"

Getting Specific: Job Responsibilities and Objectives

So far the discussion has been general. Now it gets more specific. Once you have an idea of the general job responsibilities, it's time to move on to

> ### Frequent Short Summaries
>
> In meetings, particularly those that go for an hour or two, it's a good idea to do a summary and check to make sure you both agree. Notice that's what Sharlene does before going on to identify specifics of the job tasks.

writing specific objectives. An objective is a statement of a specific result or outcome the employee is expected to create or contribute to. Objectives can also include any time or resource constraints (e.g., "by February 6" or "within allocated budget"). Here are some pointers on setting objectives:

- Make each objective as specific as possible.
- Focus each objective on a single job responsibility or outcome.
- Specify when the result should occur and any limits on resources.
- Keep the objectives short, to the point, and direct.
- Focus the objectives on results or outcomes, if possible, not on how the employee is to achieve the results.

Both the employee and the manager must understand the meaning of the objective in the same way. It should also make sense to others who might read the document. Here are examples of specific objectives:

- Catalog the library collection completely by January 28, and within the $10,000 budget.
- Respond to customer requests for information about products.
- Reduce customer wait time by 15% by the end of the year.
- Increase departmental sales by 5% without raising staff levels.

Let's return to Sharlene and Neil.

Sharlene summed up their discussion of Neil's responsibilities. "So, you have in your job description four basic responsibilities: course design, consulting directly with managers, course delivery, and supporting your teammates on projects where they could use your help. Let's go through those one by one and see if we can set some specific objectives, OK?"

Neil was ready and jumped in. "Sure. Well, under 'course design' ... We can't design courses without doing proper data analysis and needs assessment, to make sure the solutions we provide will actually address those safety problems. So, any objective is going to have to cover that, to do it right."

Objectives

Some objectives are very specific and some less so. Some sound like results and some like prescriptions for action. Sometimes it's hard to separate the two. That's OK—as long as you and the employee understand each other.

Sharlene replied: "OK. Well, we might as well take a crack at writing an objective to cover analysis and assessment. Want to take a shot?"

Neil thought for a moment and said, "How about this? Under 'course design,' we put 'Write a plan to reduce accidents and lower sick leave (by June 30), following the basic processes and standards agreed to by the branch.'"

"Sounds pretty good," Sharlene observed. "I guess that end bit means you'll be doing interviews, needs assessments, and the other things in our standard process document?"

"Yes, exactly," Neil said. "But that's not the whole thing, right? I mean, we need a strategy, so we need at least another objective about implementing the strategy."

Neil and Sharlene continued the process for each of the major job responsibility areas for Neil's position. Here are a few more objectives they agreed upon:

- Consistent with the plan, design and deliver necessary training courses (number to be determined) and evaluate their effectiveness within the budget, by December 31.

- Carry out safety audits in a timely manner for managers and departments requesting them.
- Provide assistance (upon request) to Phil, Marie, and Joe on the X, Y, and Z projects.

Developing Criteria for Success (Setting Standards)

Now comes the tough part. We need some way to determine whether the employee has succeeded in attaining the goals and objectives set. So, we need standards of performance.

Standards of performance are statements that outline what criteria will be used to determine whether the employee has met each objective. They answer such performance questions as "When?" "How good?" "How few errors?" and "To whose satisfaction?" Generally we want standards to:

- Be specific
- Be attainable with effort and "stretching"
- Be as objective and measurable as possible

You may find that if the objectives you write are very specific, the standards will be pretty much identical. Again, don't worry about getting everything perfect. The point is in the shared understanding.

Sharlene opened the transition from objectives to standards. "Well, we have a pretty good idea

> **Building in Flexibility**
>
> You might not know during the planning phase exactly what a task or a project will entail. Be as specific as possible, but keep the objective flexible. Then come back to it during the year and discuss refining it as you know more about it.

of what you need to be doing. How are we going to determine, at the end of the year, whether you've succeeded? Let's start with the workplace safety and health objectives. What do you think would be a good measure or standard?"

Neil thought for a moment. "Well," he answered, "isn't the bottom line lowering the accident rates? I mean, if what I do doesn't contribute to that, then we can't really call it a success, can we? How about a standard like "Objective will be met if accident rate falls by X% in 1999"?

Sharlene frowned, then asked, "Neil, are you sure you want to do that? You know one of the things about setting standards is that if you are going to be evaluated on something you should be in control of it. I don't see how you can be in control of accidents throughout the entire plant."

Neil responded: "Well, what's going to happen if I don't meet whatever standard we set?"

Sharlene laughed because she sensed Neil was kidding a bit. "Well, I can't see us firing you. But it is important. If we set a standard like that and then you don't meet it, we would sit down to determine why it didn't happen, where we went wrong, and how we can fix it. Basically we would have to do a proper diagnosis."

Neil came back with: "I like a challenge. I figure we should measure this by the results we want. I can live with that standard."

Sharlene ended this part of the discussion by agreeing, but she asked Neil to think about the actual reduction target, to take into account his lack of control. They agreed to finalize that standard next week. Then Sharlene moved on to another objective.

"OK, Neil, but let's consider a separate standard for the safety audit objective. How will we know whether you have achieved that objective?"

Nick replied, "Well, we don't want managers having to wait six months for me to do the audit, so maybe we should talk about turnaround time and customer satisfaction."

They continued the discussion and ended up with this standard: "Objective will be achieved if requested safety audits are completed within four weeks of the request and are considered satisfactory (no complaints) by managers involved."

Neil and Sharlene went through a similar process to set standards for the other objectives. Finally they got to the following objective: "Provide support to other staff members on projects in relevant areas of expertise."

"Well," Sharlene asked, "how do we assess that one?"

Neil thought for a moment. "Well, you said we needed to

have objective measures if we could. I suppose we could count the number of meetings I have on those projects with Phil, Marie, and Joe, or the time I spend with each of them. We could measure that. Or, we could just say that if their projects succeed, I've done my job." He paused, then added, "I don't know."

"I don't like any of those much," Sharlene admitted. "Do we really care how many meetings you have? Let me make a suggestion. How about if we ask Phil, Marie, and Joe what kind of help you can provide and see if they can set some standards for you? After all, your job is to help them with what they need—they're your "customers." I'll set up a quick meeting tomorrow and we can discuss it then. That way we'll all be on the same wavelength."

Discussion of Barriers and Help Needed

Once manager and employee set the standards, there are still a few things to deal with. Remember that our goal is to prevent problems, so the next obvious step is to discuss any difficulties, challenges, or problems that might interfere with achieving the objectives and meeting the standards. Managers can lead that discussion and also add their views.

"So, Neil," Sharlene began, "what kinds of obstacles do you see as slowing you down? And is there anything I can do to help?"

Neil hesitated. "Well, you know, I expect that there may be some resistance from the plant managers. After all, this is going to take some of their time. It would really help if we could be sure that the 'higher-ups' make it a high priority and communicate that to the other managers."

Integrating Team Issues

Some suggest that standards of performance overstress the individual's performance at the expense of team performance. Notice what Sharlene did to avoid this. Because part of Neil's role is to help members of the team, she decided to involve those people in defining what that means.

Sharlene offered to talk to the CEO and vice president in charge to enlist their support. The conversation continued, until they had discussed each of the objectives and standards and Sharlene had a short list of things she could do to help Neil.

Discussion of Priorities and Authorities

We're close to the end of the meeting. Two matters remain.

First, manager and employee have to agree on which objectives are most important and which might be less so. This is so the employee can allocate his or her time without having to consult the manager on everything. A simple way to do this is to designate a priority for each task or objective. For example, you might rate them as priority one—essential, priority two—important, and priority three—least important.

Setting priorities is a fairly straightforward process. Remember: employee and manager should do it together, so they arrive at a common understanding and the priorities reflect what the work unit and the company need.

The second matter to discuss at this point is authority. Employees need to know when they can make decisions on their own and when they need to consult the manager. For each objective, discuss the level of decision making available to the employee. You can use the following rating system:

- Complete Authority: No need to get permission or report afterward
- Act, and Then Report: Can make decision and act, but needs to report decision to manager
- Ask: Needs to get decision or permission to decide from manager

Decisions about level of authority will be affected by the ability and track record of the employee, the importance and nature of the decisions involved, what the employee needs to do the job efficiently and effectively, and what the manager needs for information or other purposes. Again, both employee and manager need to come to an understanding.

Ending the Meeting

The ending of the meeting is very important. It's a time to thank the employee, talk about how productive and useful the meeting has been, summarize key points, arrange for documentation, and plan for any follow-up to tie up loose ends. This is how Sharlene handled it.

"Well, Neil, we're pretty much done. This is hard work, but I think we are pretty much set for the year. So, thank you. You wanted to discuss how you can contribute to the team, as you mentioned at the start. I think that your revised job description and the objectives we've set for the year show how important you are to our team.

"Now, let's summarize. We both have our notes from this meeting. I'd like you to organize them and have a list of job task areas, objectives, and standards ready for next week. We'll also talk to Phil, Marie, and Joe to finish setting the standards that relate to them. What I'm going to do is list the things I can do to help you and we'll attach that to your plan, so I don't forget. We should meet to make sure we've got everything down, and then we can both sign your performance plan, so it's clear we've developed it together. As we've discussed, I'd like to talk to you every few months about your progress, and we'll use the plan to guide those discussions."

The Follow-Up

More often than not, there may be some additional work to do after the planning meeting. In our example, Sharlene and Neil need to organize their notes, consult with other employees, and finalize some standards. Those things are best done after the meeting. There's another reason to have a follow-up meeting. Between the performance planning meeting and the follow-up, new ideas or issues may crop up, stimulated by the initial conversation. It's good to allow some time to reflect before finalizing the performance plan.

An Optional Step: Action Planning

Some managers add an additional step, between the performance planning meeting and the follow-up. They ask the employee to develop an "action plan," a list of tasks or courses of action the employee intends to follow to achieve the objectives and meet the standards. At the follow-up meeting, the manager reviews the action plan with the employee. The advantage to doing this is that it makes it much easier for the employee to provide status reports during the year, since he or she can use a checklist to update the manager. The disadvantage is that it's more paperwork and time. You need to decide for yourself whether action plans are a good idea.

Manager's Checklist for Chapter 5

❑ Throughout the performance management process, focus on the communication between you and the employee. If the two of you share understanding, that's 90% of the job done.

❑ It's very difficult to write excellent objectives and standards of performance. Do your best when working with the employee. Get them as specific, objective, and measurable as you can without spending too much time getting them perfect.

❑ Your role in performance planning is to make decisions with the employee, help him or her understand what's important, and work together to set the objectives and standards.

❑ Make sure there's a process for documenting the agreements. Generally, the employee will assemble the final draft of the plan and both employee and manager will sign off. If there are ways in which you will be helping the employee, you may want to attach your commitment to the plan.

Ongoing Performance Communication

The performance management cycle starts with *planning* and ends with the *review* or *appraisal*. But what makes performance management work most effectively is what goes on between the planning and the appraisal—ongoing communication.

Take out communication and it isn't performance management. It's just planning and appraisal. Before we look at why it's so important, let's start with a definition.

Ongoing performance communication is the process by which manager and employee work together to share information about work progress, potential barriers and problems, possible solutions to problems, and how the manager can help the employee. It's a dialogue that links planning and appraisal.

The Purpose

Workplaces in the past tended to be pretty stable. People could do the same job over a year or period of years because the pace of change was slower.

That's no longer the case. The modern workplace is dynamic. The need to compete pushes companies to improve continuously. In general, the work is more complex and faster. Priorities change and the work environment changes. Barriers spring up. Managers can't assume that staff will succeed if they simply maintain the set course. One purpose of ongoing performance communication is to keep the work process dynamic, flexible, and responsive. Communication can generate changes in objectives and job tasks and new or different priorities.

Ongoing performance communication The process by which manager and employee work together to share information about work progress, potential barriers and problems, possible solutions to problems, and how the manager can help the employee. Its importance lies in its power to identify and address difficulties before they grow.

Communication helps us cope with changes. But even if there were no changes, we would need regular communication, because people need information. As a manager, you need certain information to coordinate the work of those reporting to you. You need to know the status of processes and projects so you can convey that information to your boss if necessary. You need to know whether things will be late or early. You need to avoid surprises. You need to identify potential problems early enough so you can solve them before they become more difficult. In some cases you may need information to include in the year-end performance review. And, finally, if your job is to help your staff do their jobs, you need information about how you can best help them.

Employees need information too. What's changed in terms of their priorities? Has information come to the manager that's relevant to their performance, such as customer complaints or information about defects or product errors? Some staff need more feedback and support than others, but we know that all employees need information about how they are doing to remain motivated and to improve.

So, in a nutshell, the purpose of ongoing performance communication is to make sure everybody has the information needed to improve throughout the year.

The Outcomes (Communication + Deliverables)

The details of ongoing performance communication are determined by what manager and employees need and want. Some managers want a paper trail to record progress. So, they use simple forms to track progress. Other managers want less paperwork, so they record only very significant points that must not be forgotten.

The first step in determining what and how the communication will occur is to answer the following key questions:

> **Information and Empowerment**
> *Smart Managing*
> Smart managers know that the more informed their employees are about priorities, directions, and their job tasks, the less time will be spent having to fight forest fires. Ongoing communication empowers staff to work and make decisions on their own.

- What information do I need from each employee to fulfill my responsibilities as a manager?
- What information does each employee need to fulfill his or her job responsibilities?

Ongoing communication about performance issues can help answer questions such as those in the following list. You may need some different questions answered or not need the ones we suggest. What's essential is that your communication provide answers to questions critical to success for both of you.

Here are a few questions that performance communication should allow manager and employee to answer.

- How are things going with respect to job responsibilities?
- What is going well?
- What is not going so well?
- Is the employee on track toward achieving objectives and meeting standards of performance?

- If things are not on track, what needs to change to get things on track?
- How can manager lend a hand to support improvement (even if everything is on track)?
- Has anything changed that might affect the employee's job tasks or priorities?
- If so, what changes need to be made in objectives and job tasks?

Formal Methods

Since ongoing communication about performance is vital to performance management, we need to discuss methods that will ensure that communication. You and your employees need to choose methods that don't consume too much time and don't create more work than necessary, but provide the information you need and allow the understanding that keeps you on course.

Formal methods of communication are planned and scheduled. There are three methods:
- regular written reports
- regular manager-employee meetings
- regular group or team meetings with the manager

Each method has advantages and disadvantages, which we will discuss, so you get to choose the method that best suits your situation. You might even mix and match.

Regular Written Reports

Some managers get great benefits from having employees submit regular written status reports. Unfortunately, many other managers just create huge amounts of paper and waste time.

What are the advantages of written status reports? They don't require face-to-face meetings, so they are appropriate when employees and manager are not in the same place. They provide a record, so no additional paperwork is needed.

The disadvantages? The process can easily turn into a

wasteful, pointless bureaucratic paper chase where nobody reads the reports. Few employees like doing them. Perhaps most important, written reports don't involve a dialogue between people. They're just a flow of information going one way, from employee to manager. That particular problem can be overcome by combining various methods. For example, whenever a regular

Avoiding Overload and the Paper Chase

Whether communicating in person or on paper, stay focused on what you need. A common problem in performance communication is to include too much.

For every thing discussed or reported, ask yourself, "How does this information help me or help the employee accomplish assigned job tasks?" If you have no answer, maybe there's no point in dealing with that particular bit of information.

report contains red flags or problem indicators, then the manager and the employee can get together face-to-face or by phone for problem solving. Or, monthly reports can be supplemented by a face-to-face meeting every three months so the manager and each employee can discuss performance matters and so the manager can provide feedback and information to employees, one on one.

One more disadvantage of both written reports and one-on-one meetings: Both methods involve information sharing between only two people. But what if you work in a team-based environment or any other situation where it's important that a number of people share information? Neither method meets that communication need.

Options and formats. What gets reported in regular communication is up to you. What do you need? How often do you need it? Here are some options.

You can use a brief narrative. At specified intervals, each employee produces a short summary of progress, problems encountered, and the status of the major job tasks identified during the performance planning meetings. Most managers

> ### ⚠️ CAUTION!
> ### The Paper-Shuffle Danger
> The major concern about written reports is that they tend to be seen as an unnecessary paper shuffling. If you go the written report route, it's a good idea to involve employees in determining what should be recorded and how. After all, it's additional work.

will provide some basic headings to structure the report. For example, Objective/Job Task, Status, Difficulties and Problems, and Possible Improvement Ideas or Help Needed.

You can use a structured form, with several columns. The form might include columns for employees to provide information on each of their objectives, job tasks, or standards. There might be a column for progress (on time, late, early), a column for problem identification, and so on. One advantage of a structured form? A master copy can be made for each employee, with the same objectives and job tasks listed on it. Each month, the employee simply fills in the columns on the form.

One final comment on written reports. Almost anything that can be put on paper can be transferred via electronic mail systems. That technology can be particularly useful when employees and the manager are located at different sites.

Regular Manager-Employee Meetings

Written reports do not encourage the kinds of discussions and problem solving necessary to identify problems early and to identify and implement solutions. Regularly scheduled one-on-one meetings provide those opportunities. In addition to ensuring communication, face-to-face regular meetings provide a sense of connection between manager and employee, something that can be motivating.

What are the disadvantages of regular status meetings? They can be time-consuming, particularly if not structured well. They also require some degree of interpersonal skills on the part of the manager so that communication is real, not just chitchat and cover-ups. But there are certainly ways to overcome these disadvantages.

Here are some guidelines for regular status meetings:
- Use your interpersonal skills to set the right tone for discussion and problem solving. We provide some tips for creating dialogue in the "People Techniques" section later in this chapter.
- Meetings take people away from their work. Schedule ongoing communication meetings just often enough to help staff do their jobs.
- People in certain jobs might need to meet more or less often than those in other jobs. Or, even people doing the same job may differ in terms of how much contact they need with you. You may want to handle the scheduling process on an individual basis with each employee.

> ### Open Communication
> **Smart Managing**
>
> Managers play a key role in determining whether staff will talk and share with them in an open, honest way. The key is to adopt a mind-set of problem solving, rather than blaming. When staff realize you're interested in helping them rather than blaming them, they will be much more open with you.

- It isn't usually necessary to keep elaborate notes regarding progress meetings. Generally it's a good idea to record discussions about performance deficits, actions to be taken to resolve those difficulties, and discussions about outstanding performance. Documentation of these kinds of matters is useful at year-end reviews.

Conducting the One-on-One Meeting

There are many ways to conduct ongoing performance communication meetings. Regardless of how you go about it, always keep in mind the purpose: to discuss and exchange information about job tasks so you and the employee can work together to improve. To give you a starting point, we've provided an outline of one way to conduct meetings.

Begin the meeting with a short *statement of purpose and focus*. For example: "We're here to discuss how your work is going, see if anything has changed since our last meeting, and see if there is anything that might help you carry out your job responsibilities."

Update the employee on any changes you know about that may be relevant to his or her job. For example: "It looks like the board has decided on a change of direction that might affect our work. Let me explain."

Focus on specific job tasks and standards. For example: "Let's go through the objectives and standards we set in April. I'd like to know whether you feel you're on track to meet them, and if you've come up against any problems, and what we can do to fix them." While you'll focus on getting input here, you may comment on any problems you've noticed or compliment the employee on his or her work.

Who Talks Most?

Smart Managing

While status meetings should focus on dialogue, it's a good idea to have the employee do most of the talking. Encourage self-evaluation and reporting. Then you can comment or ask questions. If problems are identified, encourage the employee to suggest solutions.

Problem solve as needed. If either of you feels something is off track, identify the reason(s) and work together to overcome the problem.

Allow room for discussion of points that might be missed by focusing on specific tasks and objectives. For example: "Now that we've talked about your specific objectives, is there anything else you feel I should know that would help me do my job better or make this place more effective?"

Record any relevant information that might be needed later. You may want to share any notes you take, particularly if they outline any agreements between the two of you.

Conclude with a summary and set a date for the next meeting. For example: "Good, now let's sum up. We've agreed you might benefit from XYZ training, so I will arrange that for you. At our next meeting in two months, we'll see whether things have gotten back on track with respect to those product defects we've discussed. Does that make sense?"

Group Meetings

The third formal method of communicating about performance occurs in a group setting. All group members meet regularly to update each other on the status of their work. Why do some workplaces use this approach? Isn't discussion of job performance something between each employee and the manager? Yes ... and no.

Obviously there are some discussions that ought to be held privately. But most routine communication about work can be shared among other employees. Should it? You have to decide.

Here's the argument. No employee is an island. Most jobs are interconnected, in some sort of system, so the work and tasks of one employee interact with the work and tasks of other employees. So, every employee can benefit from knowing and understanding what the others are doing and from participating in the joint problem-solving efforts that are often necessary.

> **⚠ CAUTION!**
>
> ## Discipline in Private
>
> When serious problems surface with respect to an individual's performance, a public forum is almost always the worst place to discuss them. Any disciplinary action should take place in private, period. Bottom line: never do anything in a group meeting that will humiliate an employee.

What about disadvantages? Two stand out: time and trouble. Time spent in meetings may be a good investment, but it's still time taken away from other tasks. Also, some people hate meetings with a passion: they'll tend to find reasons for missing them, which means more work for you. For small teams and groups, both disadvantages can be addressed through applying basic meeting management techniques and focusing tightly on the purpose of update meetings.

Conducting the Group Status Meeting

Set the focus of the meeting. Review the purpose for the meeting. For example: "We've set aside thirty minutes to update each other on our objectives, tasks, and projects. If we identify things that need to be discussed at length, we can figure out how best to do that as we go."

Each person updates. Go around the room so each person reports on significant issues, progress, and difficulties. To structure the process, whoever is chairing the meeting can use standard questions. For example:

- Can you give us a brief update on how things are going with your job responsibilities?
- What is going well?
- What kinds of challenges or problems have occurred since the last meeting?
- Is there anything any of us can do to help out?

Problem solve. If issues or problems are identified and can be dealt with quickly, do so. If not, establish a procedure to deal with the situation. You may want to schedule a smaller group meeting or ask somebody to develop a proposal.

Keep Group Meetings Short and to the Point

Provide or develop group guidelines as to how and what people should report at status meetings and the time to allot. Enforce time limits. Focus on the most important issues.

Summarize and close. After each person has spoken and the group has identified and addressed any problems or issues, close with a summary of agreements made. For example: "So, John and Mary are going to work out a method so engineers and receptionists can coordinate their work better. They'll get back to us at our meeting next month. If anyone has any suggestions, please pass them on to either of them."

Finally, it's always a good idea to produce a brief summary or minutes for meetings. Meeting participants can take turns doing that. The minutes serve as documentation, if needed later, and as a means of refreshing memories.

Informal Methods

Not all ongoing communication between manager and employees is scheduled or formalized into meetings or on paper. In fact, there's a lot of benefit in informal meetings, chats, talking during coffee breaks, or the famous "management by walking around." At one organization the staff even claimed that they got more accomplished in a twenty-minute coffee break discussion with the boss present than at any of the lengthy scheduled meetings.

The advantage of using and promoting informal methods is they are "just in time." A problem or issue occurs. A brief conversation ensues right away and things can be set straight quickly. Since problems don't occur neatly the day before scheduled meetings, you must have other means of communicating when scheduled meetings aren't "soon enough."

With informal processes, there are no "correct" ways. Some managers allocate a certain part of their day or week to dropping in on staff and asking basic questions, like "How's everything going?" or "Is there anything I can do to help you with...?" or even "Hey, you sure handled that customer well!"

> ### Rejection Kills Communication
>
> One manager complained that his staff never told him things he should know, despite his proclamation of an open-door policy. He didn't realize that the problem was his attitude: when an employee approached him, he sometimes showed disinterest or even annoyance at being interrupted. So people stopped talking to him.
>
> If you want staff to talk to you, make sure you receive visitors positively and make time for them.

One more thing. Walking around and talking informally is a good method if done with skill and sensitivity. (More on that in a moment.) What might be more important is setting a climate where employees feel comfortable coming to you when things come up. That means being clear about when you would like to be involved or consulted and making time for employees who feel a need to discuss something.

People Techniques

Despite the best of intentions, managers sometimes create situations where their approach to performance communication has negative effects. In some cases, employees feel as if the boss is interrogating them. Or, they feel that being honest results in punishment or blame or just more work. Below are a few "people techniques" to help avoid negative effects with staff, regardless of communication format.

- Focus communication on *we.* "How can we solve this problem?" "How can we make this easier?" Or better still, "How can I help?"
- Don't use questions to intimidate or bully. Use questions to get enough information on the table so you and the employee can solve the problem.
- Make sure employees understand what you need, what you want, and what to expect, so they can prepare for you. Don't assume that it's obvious.
- Don't just look at *problems,* but also at *successes.* People need to know what they're doing right, not just what they might be doing wrong. Celebrate successes as they occur.
- Encourage staff to evaluate their own progress and work. They know what's going on, because they're closer than you to their work. On occasion you may have to guide staff to a more accurate assessment. But generally most employees will be honest if they understand that you want to help them succeed, rather than to find fault.

Smart Managing

Flexibility

Pay attention to how your communication methods are working or not working. If they're not meeting your needs and the needs of your employees, change your methods.

Communication in Action

Let's close this chapter with a description of how

one manager went about the ongoing communication process. First, an important point. It has probably occurred to you that the best way to ensure communication about performance is by using several methods. Sometimes written reports might fit, but not just written reports. Regular individual meetings are good, but informal "just in time" conversations are important. Group or team meetings might work, but only if augmented by other techniques.

Sharon, as branch director, directly supervised fifteen people. When she was promoted to the job, she continued two existing formal methods for communicating with employees. First, each staff member was asked to complete a monthly update/status form and return it to her. Second, she met with each employee for about ten minutes each month to discuss his or her report. She also had a knack for establishing a very good rapport with staff and did a good deal of informal communication.

This worked for the first six months, but then the organization got busier. Getting the written reports was like pulling teeth, and each month about half of them were late. She cajoled and she used the power of her position, but the reports continued to lapse.

Sharon then did something interesting. She thought about her initial belief that everything should be documented and written down each month. And she thought about the delays and difficulties in making the reports method work. She wondered, "What is this telling me about what my staff needs from me?" Her answer was that staff didn't find the process useful and considered it a waste of time. Still, she felt she needed information regularly. Here's what she decided to do.

Sharon did away with the monthly written reports and meetings. Instead, she talked informally with people over coffee or walked around and visited them. That allowed her to stay in touch with her staff on a regular basis. She also set up short weekly staff meetings (just before the workday began) with a single purpose—to identify any issues that needed attention right away. Those meetings helped her to "red flag" potential problems early on.

Finally, she recognized that many issues required the involvement of a number of people in the organization. So she established general staff meetings for that purpose, usually at the end of every second month.

The results were positive. The new approach eliminated a lot of paperwork. When Sharon needed to document something, perhaps a success or a particular problem, she wrote basic notes. By using a combination of methods and by showing that she was working with the staff, she created a situation where she got better, more timely information when she needed it, while reducing unnecessary work.

> **Smart Managing**
>
> ### Use Multiple Approaches
>
> Don't rely on a single communication approach. All have advantages and disadvantages. Use a combination of methods that meet both your needs and the needs of your staff.

Manager's Checklist for Chapter 6

❏ Choose the best combination of methods for communicating about performance. Begin by answering these two questions: "What information do I need to do my job and when do I need it?" and "What information do my employees need to do their jobs and when do they need it?"

❏ To promote an open, nonthreatening climate, explain the reasons for ongoing communication about performance and invite staff to suggest useful and efficient ways to do it.

❏ Aim all communication at identifying and solving problems, not blaming.

❏ Ongoing performance communication is a dynamic process. Modify your methods according to your situations—and your results. Customize to meet the needs of each employee.

Data Gathering, Observing, and Documenting

If we see performance management as a problem-solving process, does it make sense to go by gut feeling? Are you prepared to discipline employees or give pay raises because you just feel as if they deserve it? Or, if you're trying to work with employees to help them improve, does it make sense to send them to a dozen training courses in the hope that something might work? If that's the best you can do, you'll waste resources—and maybe not even improve performance.

For all those decisions, you need data. And you need a way of recording data and the decisions you make. That's what we're going to cover in this chapter.

Data gathering is an organized, systematic way to collect information about the performance of an employee, the work unit, or the organization. For example, you might have customers complete brief feedback forms, or you might count the number of widgets produced that need to be redone or fixed before they are shipped, or you might look at turnaround time, the time required to process orders.

Observation is a special kind of data gathering. It's what

you as a manager see or hear. If you hear an employee being rude to a customer, that's observation. If someone tells you an employee was mean to a customer, that's not observation, because you didn't see it or hear it yourself. When we talk about reasons for gathering information and observing, you'll see why this distinction is important.

Data gathering An organized, systematic way to collect information about performance, generally by measuring something.

Observation A special kind of data gathering, when a manager sees or hears something directly, not from somebody else.

Finally, documenting refers to the actions a manager takes to record and keep track of data gathering, observations, and communication and decisions involving individual employees.

Why Do We Gather Data and Observe?

You don't have time to collect data for the fun of it. Nobody does. And if you spend your time hovering over staff, watching them work, they get mighty tired of feeling as if buzzards are circling. Not to mention you probably have other things to do. So, let's look at why you need data and why you might need to observe staff.

Documenting Recording and keeping track of information so it doesn't get lost and is available when needed. The information might include data, your observations, and records of your discussions with individual staff on performance issues.

We collect data and observe performance to solve problems. To solve a problem, we need to know two things—that a problem exists and what might be causing the problem. So we need information.

And sometimes, to convince someone that there's a problem, you need hard information, information that goes beyond the "maybe, sometimes, it's possible you could be doing better" approach.

There's another reason why we need data and observations. It has to do with legal issues and protection from unwarranted charges by employees. As we mentioned earlier in this book, you have to abide by labor laws and labor agreements applicable to your company and location. If you take disciplinary action because of performance problems, you need evidence that a problem exists and that you've communicated the problem to the employee in question. Your opinion may not be enough to protect you. Specific, actual observations and data will more than likely allow you to justify your actions. The protection isn't only one-sided. The requirement for data and details also protects employees.

Reasons for Data Gathering, Observing, and Documenting

We can summarize the main reasons for data gathering, observing, and documenting as follows:

- To provide an ongoing fact-based record of both positives and negatives of employee performance to be used in decision making.
- To identify potential problems as early as possible so they can be addressed and the employee can improve.
- To identify employee strengths so they can be developed further and then deployed most effectively.
- To enhance employee motivation through recognition of good work.
- To collect enough accurate information to solve problems.
- To record specifics of performance and communication about performance, to be used in disciplinary actions and related grievances or potential legal complaints.

What Do We Gather? What Do We Document?

You could become a data junkie, picking up information and recording it like a manic stamp collector. But that's not wise. Data collection takes time, effort, and money. The more data you collect, the more resources you need to make sense of it, to use it. Making sense of data isn't a trivial process.

What you gather will depend in part on the goals and objectives of your organization. If your unit provides a service to customers, for example, then gathering customer satisfaction information is useful. Although we can't tell you what data will be useful to your organization as a whole or what data will help you and your employees during the performance management process, we can offer some suggestions.

We'll focus mostly on information related to performance management. But keep in mind that performance management is only a part of the continuous improvement process. Consider gathering information for the following purposes:

- To determine instances of great or poor performance (e.g., widgets produced by each worker, number of faulty widgets, customer complaints, customer praise).
- To identify the causes of performance problems. (Do employees have trouble making only certain widgets? Or only when they have to go fast? Do they receive customer complaints only when under stress? From women? From men?)
- To ascertain the factors behind excellent performance. (Managers never seem to think about that purpose!) By finding out how your best employees work, you may be able to use that information to help others doing similar jobs do better. Benchmark your best performers.
- To provide evidence to determine whether your employees have achieved their objectives and standards. In other words, the data you collect is determined by the standards you set with staff.

Where do you get the information? Again, it depends on what you need. But information can come from many sources:

- Direct customers
- Executives
- Employees
- Yourself (manager)
- Employees and managers in other departments in your company that interact with your department and employees
- Suppliers

Now you have a general idea of what sorts of data you can collect and where you can collect it. The next question is: "What do I document?" With respect to performance management itself, you're probably going to document or track:

- records of achievement (of lack of achievement) of objectives and standards
- praise and critical comments received about an employee's behavior or work
- specific evidence needed to substantiate either inferior work or superior work
- any other data that will help you and employee identify causes of problems (or successes)
- records of any performance-related conversations you have with an employee, which you should have the employee sign if the issue is serious
- critical incident data

That last item, "critical incident data," generally refers to relatively extreme behavior—usually negative, such as arriving at work drunk, swearing at a customer, yelling, harassing fellow employees, or theft. As you can imagine, some critical incidents might be grounds for immediate dismissal.

When these incidents occur, it's best to record as much information as possible, as soon as possible. For example, an employee arrives at work smelling of liquor and slurring words. You should record date, time of contact, any discussions that ensued at that time, details of employee behavior, and how the incident was handled. The report is usually in the form of a little narrative, a story of the event. As they used to say on *Dragnet*, "just the facts." Describe what happened as best you can. Don't embellish or interpret. Finally, in very serious situations, you might ask any third parties who witnessed the incident to submit a report.

> **Key Term**
>
> **Critical incident**
> Behavior that is usually extreme (either very good or bad) and that should be recorded for legal reasons, for disciplinary measures, or for purposes of recognizing exemplary actions "above and beyond the call of duty."

A Positive Critical Incident

A man enters a convenience store and tells the clerk to hand over the money in the till. Rather than give in, the employee tackles the would-be thief (it's a dangerous but instinctive reaction). If you're the store manager, you'd want to document this action in a critical incident report. Why? First, your head office will want one. It helps management improve store safety. Second, you might want to commend this employee—even though you want to discourage taking such a risk.

Critical incident reports are vital if serious actions are necessary (dismissal or legal action). They also provide evidence that you're exercising due diligence by addressing serious problems as they occur or come to your attention. This is particularly important in areas such as harassment.

Where Does Performance-Related Documentation Go?

What should you do with all those documents? Employees want to make sure there's a permanent record of the positive stuff—any commendations, successes, or customer praise. However, they aren't so comfortable having every little mistake they make recorded and sent to sit forever and ever in their personnel files in the human resources department. Managers have to make some tough decisions.

Let's say you have some information to show that an employee's production has dropped off. It's worth discussing with the employee. You want to stop the trend if you can. If you document the information, and the results of your meeting with the employee, do you send it along to the permanent file? Some managers do and some don't.

Those who do suggest that the information may be important down the road if performance problems recur again, particularly if the employee ends up working in another part of the organization. There's some logic to that approach to documentation.

Managers who prefer not to enter "transient" information into permanent files feel that they should first try to solve the problem with the employee. That way, employees get some period of time to correct the problem (with help from the manager), before it's considered serious enough to keep in a permanent record. Managers will broach the subject like this: "Fred, we've identified a problem here, and I think we should see if we can solve it over the next three months. If your production doesn't come up to the standard you and I agreed on in our last planning meeting, then we'll have to make note of it in your record. If we get it solved, there's no reason to keep a record of it, since it's no longer a problem."

This approach seems fairer and more tolerant. Decisions about what you put into the permanent record will depend on the seriousness of the issue, company policy on personnel files, your personal comfort levels, and what seems most likely to develop good long-term relationships with your staff.

Hints and Tips

So much of what you do with data gathering, observing, and documenting depends on your specific situation and company policy. Let's end this chapter with some hints and tips.

Data gathering can't be your responsibility alone. You'll have to trust your staff to help. For example, you might observe telephones ringing ten or twenty times. But what does that tell you? There *may* be a problem. The only way to assess the seriousness of the problem is to find out how often it occurs and how long callers must wait for an answer. You can't stand there for hours every day counting the rings, can you?

If you enlist the help of staff in gathering that data, you've done two things. You've found a practical means of examining the problem—and you've involved employees in the problem-solving process, so they don't feel as if it's just you checking up on them.

Gather data for a purpose. Don't fall prey to "data fever," collecting data without knowing why or how it will be used. Some companies go so far as to have regular surveys and have employees keep track of everything, and then do nothing with the data they collect. That can get awfully expensive and wasteful. Always determine why you need information you collect and how it will be used before you collect it.

Summarize your data simply and appropriately. That's often a challenge for managers. Unless you're skilled in using the tools of quality improvement, total quality management, or other statistically based approaches, keep it simple. Tally sheets are great for counting different things. Certain kinds of graphs are useful to summarize data and see patterns.

Distinguish between what you *observe* and what you *infer*. This distinction is very important. For example, you might see an employee banging a fist on the desk. That's an *observation*. If you say, "He was absolutely furious and out of control," that's an *inference*. You're using your observation to speculate about his emotional state. You may be really good at making inferences—but unless you're 100% accurate, you'll never know when you're right or when you're wrong. So remember the distinction and document only what you *observe*.

This is particularly important if the documentation is used in a legal proceeding. If you put, "He was absolutely furious and out of control," an attorney or judge will ask how you knew that. And if you can't provide sufficient evidence for your "knowledge," it's just an interpretation and that's a real problem. Stick to the facts. Even "She arrived drunk" is an inference. The facts might be "She slurred words, smelled of alcohol, and bumped into several pieces of furniture." Some medical conditions can mimic the symptoms of drunkenness. Imagine the legal problems if you infer wrong and fire an employee who has a medical condition.

> **TRICKS OF THE TRADE**
>
> ## Simple or Complex?
>
> In general, keep data gathering and summarizing as simple as possible so everyone can take part.
>
> Some companies provide advanced training in data-gathering methods and summary techniques, like graphing and simple statistics. That can be beneficial, but it's not necessary.
>
> What you collect and how you summarize it should be no more complex than needed to suit your specific business purposes.

Use sampling to reduce the amount of data or information you need to collect. Do you need to count the number of rings before each and every telephone call is answered to measure response time? No. Take a representative sample. You could look at only 5% of the phone calls to get an approximation. The key, though, is to make it *representative*.

Let's say you need information to evaluate whether the receptionist is meeting the set standard and find ways to reduce response time. You decide to count rings before the phone is answered. Do you use one phone call a day for a week as your sample? No, that's not enough. Do you count the first thirty calls of the day for a week? No good. The call volume could be particularly high early in the morning, so response time would not be *representative*. So you might count rings for every tenth call every day for a different week each month. That would probably be representative. If calls increase seasonally, your data gathering should reflect that circumstance, if appropriate to your purposes for the data.

Manager's Checklist for Chapter 7

❏ Data gathering, observing, and documenting allow you to base performance management and improvement on facts rather than feelings.

❏ Documentation ensures that important information doesn't get lost. It's also important for legal reasons. Disciplinary action without proper documentation can be very costly.

❏ The methods you use to collect data and what you collect will depend on your context and your purposes. Gathering data without understanding why you are doing so and how you will use it can be worse than collecting nothing.

❏ It's impossible for a manager to be responsible for all information gathering, and it's foolish to try. Every staff member can collect data and observe, so everyone can help solve problems and contribute to continuous improvement.

Three Approaches to Evaluating Performance

If there were one perfect method of evaluating performance, life would be much easier. There isn't. Nobody has invented a perfect way, although people keep trying. Sometimes it seems as if newer, more complicated approaches to performance appraisal are worse than the more basic ones! Regardless, each approach has advantages and disadvantages, so the key is to recognize the limitations of the system you're using and work around them as much as possible.

In this chapter we'll examine three of the more common approaches to performance appraisal, assess the merits of each, and provide some tips on making them work. If you're in a position to build a performance management system from scratch, this chapter will help you decide which approach or combination of approaches would make sense in your workplace. If you're required to use a particular approach, you may want to augment it with parts from another approach.

Before we look at rating systems, ranking systems, and objective-based systems, we should define a term we've used in earlier chapters: "performance appraisal." Performance appraisal is the process by which an individual's work performance is assessed and evaluated. It answers the basic question, "How well has the employee performed during the period of time in question?" It's just one part of performance management, not the whole. Performance management also involves planning, diagnosing problems, identifying barriers to performance, and working to develop staff.

Why is the distinction important? Because appraisal, by itself, will not prevent problems. If you think yearly evaluation meetings with employees will cause significant improvement, you'll be disappointed.

> **Performance appraisal**
> The process by which an individual's work performance is assessed and evaluated. It answers the question, "How well has the employee performed during the period of time in question?" It's only a part of performance management.

The Dilemma of Individual Performance Appraisal

Most of us live in an individualistic culture. We value, respect, admire, and reward individuals who accomplish great things. When people succeed, we give them credit. When people do badly, we tend to blame them. In an individualistic culture, we place responsibility for success or failure on the individual.

Is this emphasis a good thing or a bad thing? Let's leave that question to the philosophers. What we need to consider here is whether job performance is determined only by individual effort and skill. If so, we can feel comfortable evaluating individual performance and rewarding and/or punishing each employee. However, if job performance is determined by the individual plus other factors (people, resources, systems), then we need to consider those other factors if we want to improve. Which is it?

We could discuss management theory to decide the issue. But let's use our own experience and good sense instead. Consider the following situations:

- The best opera singer in the world performs with an amateur orchestra and conductor. The opera singer does her best, but the performance is terrible. Do we blame the opera singer? Or do we praise her efforts?
- The best basketball player of all time moves to the worst team in the league. Although he scores over fifty points every game, the team loses 85% of its games. Do we applaud the star player? Or do we recognize that the team has failed?
- An auto assembly line has to be shut down periodically because of shortages of material. As a result, production is lower than expected. How do we evaluate the workers?
- A manager of a retail store is told to increase store sales by 20% or be terminated. At the same time his staffing budget is cut, resulting in a sloppy store, long lines at the cash register, and customer dissatisfaction. Sales drop. Does it make sense to fire the manager? More important, would hiring a new manager improve store sales?

Do you see the problem? The opera singer, the basketball player, the assembly line workers, the retail store manager: no matter how good or even great their individual efforts may be, there's a performance problem. If you focus only on the individual, you cannot solve those problems—or perhaps even determine the real cause of the problems.

None of us is an island. Our performances are determined by some individual factors, like skill and effort, but also by factors beyond our direct control—decisions made by others, resources allotted to us, the system in which we work, and so on. If we evaluated the retail store manager above, for example, we'd conclude that he'd failed. If the head office replaced him, the new manager would fail. And the next manager and the next manager. Not only is that unfair, it's just stupid. The company would be firing people who are probably good managers. Most important, by attributing the poor sales to the managers, the company will never identify the real reason why the store is going down the tubes.

So here's the dilemma. Our culture and our companies require that we evaluate employee performance on an individual basis. If we focus on individual performance and don't look at the context, the conditions that limit performance, then our efforts will fail. We won't improve because we won't

> **⚠ CAUTION!**
> **Appraisals Are Just the Beginning**
> Whatever method you use to assess performance, it's important to avoid two traps.
> First, don't assume that performance problems occur in isolation or are "always the employee's fault." Second, no assessment will give a complete picture of what is happening and why. It's a starting point for further discussion and diagnosis.

see real causes. We may punish people for things beyond their control. We may reward the wrong people for the wrong reasons.

What's the solution? It's in the mind-set. Although you may be required to evaluate each employee, keep in mind that individual performance is not completely (or even mostly) under the control of the employee. If you see performance appraisal as a tool to improve, rather than some final judgment, you're more likely to identify real problems and avoid blaming or rewarding people for things not under their control. Then everybody can gain.

We're going to discuss three methods of performance appraisal—rating, ranking, and objective-based. But whatever their advantages and disadvantages, remember that all individual performance appraisal approaches have the same limitations. When we assess individual performance, we must always consider the context and do a proper diagnosis of why problems are occurring and not jump to conclusions.

Rating Systems

Rating systems are very common—perhaps the most popular way to assess performance. That may be because ratings require the least effort. But they may not be the best way to evaluate staff. The question we need to answer is, "How much value do they add to the organization and to what extent do they help create improvement and success?"

Rating systems can be best described as "workplace report cards," much like the ones teachers in elementary schools use for their students. They consist of two parts: a list of characteristics, areas, or behaviors to be assessed and some scale or other way to indicate the level of performance on each item.

The "scale part" is like the elementary school grading system (e.g., A, B, C, D, F), except it may use numbers or phrases instead of letters. Where letters or numbers are used, they're usually associated with points along a scale (e.g., never, seldom, most of the time, always). You're probably familiar with the approach, but Table 8-1 shows some examples of job criteria and scales.

Performance Criterion Statements	Scale			
1. Completes work on time.	Never 1	Sometimes 2	Usually 3	Always 4
2. Demonstrates skills and abilities needed to do job.	Not Consistently 1	Consistently 2		Always 3
3. Demonstrates creativity and initiative.	Never 1	Sometimes 2	Usually 3	Always 4
4. Meets or exceeds sales targets each quarter.	Room for Improvement 1	Satisfactory 2		Excellent 3

Table 8-1. Some sample items often used in rating systems

Typical Usage

Most companies using rating systems do so to bring some uniformity and consistency to the performance appraisal process. Typically the human resources or personnel department will provide managers with a standard form—a "one size

fits all" approach, so
everyone in the company
is assessed in a similar
way. Once a year man-
agers are asked (or re-
quired) to submit a com-
pleted rating form for
personnel files. Some
companies ask that all
the appraisals be done at
the same time (such as
at the end of the fiscal

**Sample Criteria
Used in Rating Staff**
• Completes tasks on sched-
ule
• Shows initiative and creativity
• Interacts with clients in a polite,
constructive way
• Demonstrates a high level of organi-
zation
• Meets or exceeds sales targets each
quarter

year), while others use the hiring anniversary date of each
employee. In many cases, managers must use the forms given
to them.

Who does the ratings? It varies. Some managers simply
rate the employees. Other managers ask employees to rate
themselves and use those ratings. Others will both rate the
employees and ask employees to self-rate, and then compare
the two assessments and arrive at some compromise assessment. However the ratings are determined, both the manager
and the employee sign the completed form.

Of course there are many variations in the nuts-and-bolts
process. Sometimes managers are permitted to use their own
forms and criteria.

Strengths of Rating Systems

Rating systems are so popular because it's possible to complete the rating obligations quickly and with a minimum of effort. A manager can complete a typical rating form in ten to
fifteen minutes and send it on, satisfying the requirements set
by the human resources folks. Most employees and managers
are familiar with the "report card" approach, so they don't
seem to need any training to use the system. It's simple and
intuitive—at least at first glance. Finally, it allows a single system to be used across jobs and departments, a standardization that appeals to human resources departments.

Weaknesses of Rating Systems

The most important weakness of rating systems comes, ironically, from their strength. Since rating systems appear easy to use, simple, and standardized, it's easy for managers to forget why they're doing them and just get them out of the way. A manager can complete a rating form in ten to fifteen minutes, but if that's all a manager is doing, chances are more harm than benefit will result. That's because our aim should be not to just complete the form, but to work with employees to improve performance. No form is going to help us do that by itself. Simple rating systems help managers forget the point.

Focusing on the Form

If you focus too much on completing the form, you are probably wasting your time and risk making things worse. What's important is not the completed form, but how you go about working with each employee, discussing performance, diagnosing performance, and improving performance. Ratings are just a way of beginning discussions in partnership with staff.

Let's ask some other questions about rating systems.

First, do they give some objective assessments of performance that manager and employee would easily agree upon? Generally not. The criteria used (as in the examples in Table 8-1) are usually vague and imprecise. Will any two people agree on the meaning of "demonstrates creativity and initiative"? No. What happens?

Appraisals get bogged down in arguments between manager and employee because the criteria are vague. It becomes unpleasant, which is one reason why managers and employees come to loathe the process. Even the scales used can be vague or unclear. What does "sometimes" mean? How about "consistently"?

Another question: Do rating systems provide feedback specific enough to help employees improve their performance? Again, generally not, at least not by themselves. For example, assume that an employee is rated as "sometimes" (below average) on "creativity and initiative." Does that tell the employee how to improve? Take a course, or work harder, or be more aggressive or maybe less aggressive? The rating doesn't tell us how to fix the problem. Also, consider that a yearly rating system isn't timely enough to help employees improve. Rating once a year focuses on looking in the rear-view mirror, rather than solving or preventing problems.

Do rating systems protect employers from legal action? Often not. While rating systems may meet the requirement that performance problems be communicated to staff, the use of vague job assessment criteria may not be defensible. For example, what about an employee

> **Clarify What It Means** TRICKS OF THE TRADE
>
> If you have to use ratings, always clarify the meaning of each item in advance. Involve staff in determining what each item means. This established common meaning and avoids squabbling later on.

who often comes to work late? Is a rating of "poor" sufficient documentation to convince a court that the disciplinary action taken is fair and based on objective, valid reasons? Unlikely. The court will probably want much more specific information, such as dates or total amount of time late. We need to be careful about assuming that rating systems protect. In many situations, they create a false sense of security.

Are there other issues to consider? Yes, but rather than go through them one by one, let's use the criteria for a performance management process that works, as outlined in Chapter 2. We've summarized the key criteria and comments in Table 8-2.

In Summary

Rating systems are quite common, but the process is flawed if ratings are the only method used to appraise and manage performance. Ratings aren't helpful in planning performance, preventing problems, protecting the organization, or developing

Criteria	Comments
Helps organizations coordinate work of units and helps align individual jobs with larger goals	Not by itself. Doesn't focus on job tasks.
Helps identify barriers to success that interfere with an organization's productivity	Often not used to identify and remove barriers, but can serve as a beginning point for problem solving.
Provides ways of documenting and communicating about performance that conform to legal requirements	Probably not. Can give a false sense of security. Criteria often too vague to stand up to legal challenge.
Provides valid information to use for decisions about promotions, employee development, and training	Not by itself. Ratings alone give little concrete information, but may be used as a basis for generating more valid information.
Provides a cooperative forum to identify problem areas, diagnose problems, and eliminate barriers to individual success	Tends to create arguments because it's vague. Needs to be augmented by detailed discussion to serve these purposes.
Helps manager coordinate the work of all people reporting to him or her	No. Focuses mostly on appraisal rather than planning or coordination.
Provides regular, ongoing feedback that improves employee motivation	Not if it's a once-a-year process.
Prevents mistakes by making expectations clear and establishing shared understanding and authority levels	No. Focuses on looking backward, not forward. Needs to be augmented to serve this purpose.
Is simple to do and practical	The system is so easy that it encourages superficiality.
Involves minimal paperwork and bureaucracy	Depends on how it's implemented.
Serves the needs of managers, employees, and the organization	Generally not. Employees, in particular, dislike the process and find it a waste of time.
Time needed to do it is practical	Ratings can be done very quickly. The faster they are done, the more useless they are.

Table 8-2. Summary evaluation of a rating system

employees because they're too vague. What can you do if your company requires you to use a rating system? How can you avoid the problems and compensate for the flaws?

Keep in mind that effective performance management is

about people, relationships, and creating mutual understanding. If your company hands you a tool that isn't very good, use other ones to support and augment it. Great managers will make even a lousy system work because they expand on it, use it as a starting point for what's important, which is the relationship and communication between manager and employee.

Tips for Making Rating Systems Work

Here are some ways you might make rating systems work to improve performance.

- Supplement the rating system with regular discussions with each employee about how work is going. Do not wait until the yearly review to discuss any problems.
- Supplement the rating sheet or form with some way of making short comments about each item. If the rating is low, explain why. If it's high, explain what the person has done well.
- Always clarify the meaning of each rating item before doing the rating. Discuss your idea of its meaning and ask the employee about how he or she understands it.
- Rate together with each employee. Negotiate the ratings to reach common ground when possible. Involve staff in the discussion. Don't just render judgments.
- Don't stop with just the rating. Regardless of how you rate an item, a great question to ask is, "What do you feel you need to improve on this over the next year?" Another one is, "What can I or the two of us do to help you improve?"
- Always keep in mind that most ratings are subjective, based on opinion, and they cannot measure performance exactly. Take them seriously, but not too seriously.
- If you are ordered to use a rating system, supplement it with various tools taken from more objective approaches. There are good ways to prepare staff for evaluation meetings. Interpersonal skills can help place you and the employee on the same side. Diagnostic techniques can ensure that you're not looking just at individual performance but also at barriers in the system. Using such

skills and techniques, you can work around the basic flaws in the rating approach.

Ranking Systems

Ranking systems involve comparing people against each other and determining whether an employee is better than, the same as, or worse than his or her colleagues on the basis of some set of criteria (e.g., sales totals or management ability).

The difference between rating (using standards) and ranking (making comparisons) is significant. What if you manage an exceptionally able staff? You could *rate* all of them high—but you'd have to *rank* one of them as "best" (however that's defined) and one of them as "worst." Likewise, if you have a terrible staff, someone—no matter how poor the performance—is going to be ranked at the top.

The only reason we've included ranking systems in this discussion is to encourage you not to use them. They're almost never appropriate.

Why not? To explain, let's consider unwanted side effects. You know that almost any medication has some side effects. But we use it if the benefits outweigh the risks of undesirable side effects. On the other hand, if the

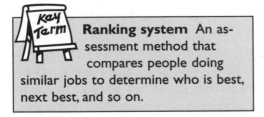

Ranking system An assessment method that compares people doing similar jobs to determine who is best, next best, and so on.

benefits of a medication are outweighed by very severe side effects, we might be wise to avoid using it.

Ranking systems have the potential to cause unwanted side effects. Because ranking systems compare colleagues, in a very real sense they push people to compete with each other. There are two ways for an employee to be ranked higher than his or her colleagues. One is to perform better and accomplish more. That's not bad. The second way is for the employee to make sure that his or her colleagues (competitors) perform worse and accomplish less. That's bad.

In the short run, ranking systems can encourage some people to work harder to come out on top. But they can also encourage people to passively or actively interfere with the work of others. Sounds cynical? It happens—and not just with selfish, nasty, unethical employees. It happens when employees get focused on a single goal and don't pay attention to other important goals. Rankings encourage that. That's not in the interests of the organization, since we want everyone to do well. We don't want to reward some people simply or primarily because other people are doing poorly.

Rank Rankings

Selling houses is a tough business. There's big money in commissions, but the competition is stiff.

ABC Realty decided to award a bonus to the salesperson who sold the most property. Every quarter, the boss released the individual sales figures, ranked the reps, and rewarded the top dog. What happened? Some harmful side effects.

The reps started doing only the things that would help them come out on top. They didn't do their paperwork. Phone messages were misrouted—or just "got lost." They competed for each new client, almost skulking around the phones to pounce on calls. They stopped cooperating. Morale dropped. Arguments became more common and much more intense.

Over the short term, some of the reps sold more. Over the long term, however, the company as a whole was less successful.

In Summary

Ranking systems, particularly those tied to monetary rewards, provide incentive for employees to want their colleagues to perform less well. They also suffer from many of the flaws of rating systems. The criteria are often vague. While rankings can be based on objective measures, often the rankings are very subjective. Table 8-3 summarizes some of the issues in using ranking systems.

Criteria	Comments
Helps organizations coordinate work of units and helps align individual jobs with larger goals	Not by itself. Doesn't focus on job tasks.
Helps identify barriers to success that interfere with an organization's productivity	No. Its focus on comparing employees may result in missing barriers that exist for every employee.
Provides ways of documenting and communicating about performance that conform to legal requirements	Only in the rare situation where ranking is based on a single, measurable criterion.
Provides valid information to use for decisions about promotions, employee development, and training	Maybe. But only when ranking is based on a single, measurable criterion. Rankings based on "fuzzy" criteria are too subjective.
Provides timely information to managers so they can prevent problems	No, certainly not if it's only a once-a-year process and ignored the rest of the time. Focus is not on *improving*, just on *comparing*.
Provides a cooperative forum to identify problem areas, diagnose problems, and eliminate barriers to individual success	Tends to create arguments because it's vague. Pushes staff to compete with each other, which may not be good for the company.
Helps manager coordinate the work of all people reporting to him or her	No. Focuses mostly on *appraisal* rather than planning or coordination.
Provides regular, ongoing feedback that improves employee motivation	Not if it's a once-a-year process.
Prevents mistakes by making expectations clear and establishing shared understanding and authority levels	No. Focuses on looking backward, not forward. Needs to be augmented to serve this purpose.
Is simple to do and practical	The system is so easy that it encourages superficiality.
Involves minimal paperwork and bureaucracy	Depends on how it's implemented.
Serves the needs of managers, employees, and the organization	Generally not. Many employees are not comfortable being compared rather than evaluated individually.
Time needed to do it is practical	Rankings can be done very quickly. The faster they are done, the more useless they are.

Table 8-3. Summary evaluation of a ranking system

Appraisal by Objectives and Standards

By now you've probably realized that we believe the best way to evaluate or appraise performance is through the use of objectives, standards, or targets. We've suggested that performance planning should involve setting targets for each employee. We've suggested that ongoing communication should focus on progress toward achieving those targets, identifying barriers, and removing them. Now, we're going to suggest that using individual targets is the better way to assess performance. Is it perfect? No. No perfect system exists.

While rating systems assess a person's performance by some usually vague criterion and ranking systems compare a person's performance against the performance of others, appraisal by objectives measures a person's performance according to a set of standards or targets negotiated individually with each person. As we pointed out in Chapter 5, the objectives and standards set during performance planning are written to be measurable in some objective way. They are set individually to allow some flexibility that reflects the level of development and ability of each employee.

Typical Usage

As we described in Chapter 5, during the performance planning process the manager sits down with each employee to agree upon objectives, targets, and standards. During the appraisal meeting, usually at the end of a one-year period, manager and employee examine each of the targets or standards and determine whether the employee has achieved those goals. If the targets and standards are clear and well understood, then the process usually goes fairly smoothly. The important point, though, is that in an objective-based system the appraisal meeting isn't just for appraisal. It provides the basis for the manager and employee to discuss any performance that did not meet the objectives, to diagnose any problems, and to come up with ideas for minimizing those problems.

Advantages

Let's go through some of the advantages of an objective-based system.

- It allows easy linking of individual objectives to work unit objectives.
- It reduces the likelihood of disagreement during appraisal meetings—if standards and targets were written well during the performance planning process.
- It's more likely to put manager and employee on the same side, unlike ranking or rating systems.
- It's probably the most legally defensible approach to appraisal.

Disadvantages

No approach is perfect. What are the disadvantages of an objective-based system?

- It takes more time than rating or ranking systems, because of the need to invest in up-front performance planning.
- It requires managers and employees to develop skills in writing objectives and standards that are meaningful and measurable.
- It may result in more paperwork than rating and ranking systems.
- Like any system, it can be misused or used in a superficial way by managers who lose track of why they are doing it.

Table 8-4 includes more things to consider about using this system.

⚠ CAUTION!

Undesirable Side Effects

There may be a risk of side effects associated with any approach to performance management. When you decide how to manage and appraise performance, it's always smart to involve staff in the development of the approach. This will help you identify side effects that you might not consider. Employees may see problems you could miss.

In Summary

Objective-based appraisal methods require more of manager and employee than ratings and rankings do. Both

Criteria	Comments
Helps organizations coordinate work of units and helps align individual jobs with larger goals	Yes, because it stresses planning as well as appraisal.
Helps identify barriers to success that interfere with an organization's productivity	Yes, when integrated as part of the complete performance management system. This benefit depends on the manager's attitude.
Provides ways of documenting and communicating about performance that conform to legal requirements	Probably the most legally defensible approach.
Provides valid information to use for decisions about promotions, employee development, and training	Yes, provided that targets are written well, which takes skill on part of manager and employee.
Provides timely information to managers so they can prevent problems	Yes, provided that it's integrated into the overall system and the principle of "no surprises" is respected.
Provides a cooperative forum to identify problem areas, diagnose problems, and eliminate barriers to individual success	Depends on interpersonal abilities of manager and employee to create that forum. Since the process is a partnership from the start, cooperation for appraisal is more likely.
Helps manager coordinate the work of all people reporting to him or her	Yes, when done properly.
Provides regular, ongoing feedback that improves employee motivation	Not if it's a once-a-year process. But even then it makes it easier to discuss progress related to objectives throughout the year.
Prevents mistakes by making expectations clear and establishing shared understanding and authority levels	Yes, that's the key—clarity.
Is simple to do and practical	No, it's not simple. Yes, it can be practical.
Involves minimal paperwork and bureaucracy	Depends on how it's implemented. Tends to result in more paperwork than other methods.
Serves the needs of managers, employees, and the organization	When done properly.
Time needed to do it is practical	It's practical if it's understood as an investment. More time up front saves time later.

Table 8-4. Summary evaluation of an objective-based system

manager and employee need some skills and need to put in the time. Rating and ranking systems allow easy, superficial appraisals that may be worth little or nothing at all. Objective-based systems demand a greater investment and yield a far better return.

Manager's Checklist for Chapter 8

❏ Choosing among appraisal methods involves understanding the advantages and disadvantages of each and understanding the potential costs and potential benefits of different approaches.

❏ Any method can have undesirable side effects, particularly if it's used without proper thought and care. Be alert to potential problems with your appraisal system and encourage staff to help identify problems. In other words, evaluate the evaluation system each year.

❏ Rating and ranking systems share a common problem. They often use evaluation criteria that are vague. That's the basic problem. If you're stuck with such a system, the "workaround" is to make sure employees understand the criteria before you use the system.

❏ Objective- or target-based systems can be made much less vague, but it takes skill on the part of manager and employee to make the targets useful for appraisal.

The Performance Appraisal Meeting

It's that time of year at the ABC Corporation. It's the time employees walk on eggshells and managers wish they dug ditches for a living. (Ah, the simplicity!) It's performance appraisal time. One by one, grumpy employees meet with grumpy managers. A very few leave the meetings less grumpy than when they entered. Most emerge even grumpier.

Performance appraisal grumpiness is really a symptom. And it's pretty normal. Even though it's common, it isn't benign. It causes managers to avoid or delay performance appraisal meetings, or to handle them in superficial ways. It causes employees to be wary and anxious, and perhaps less than honest. It's a bit of a self-fulfilling prophecy. If managers and employees are uncomfortable with the process, they're less likely to make it work.

Does it have to be this way? No. The reason why performance appraisal meetings cause so much avoidance and anxiety is that managers and employees approach them with the wrong mind-set and often use the wrong process. While it may not be possible to reduce appraisal anxiety to zero, you can make huge strides in making it more valuable to your employees and, by extension, to you as their manager. In this chapter we'll help you set up and conduct appraisal meetings so they add value and so they can be used as effective tools to improve performance.

Let's talk first about terminology. For most people, the three terms "performance appraisal," "performance evaluation," and "performance review" mean the same thing. Generally, they refer to a meeting, usually held once a year, where manager and employee discuss employee performance, document progress (success and problems), and apply a problem-solving process to overcome problems in the present and the future.

> **Key Term**
>
> **Performance appraisal, performance review, performance evaluation** Three terms, often used interchangeably, to describe the annual meeting where manager and employee discuss employee performance, document progress (success and problems), and apply a problem-solving approach to overcome problems in the present and the future.

What Makes the Process Work?

Before we talk about the specifics of the process, we'll share a secret with you. If you treat performance management as a complete system, not leaving out any of the parts, and if you succeed with performance planning and ongoing performance communication, we can almost guarantee success during the performance appraisal or review meetings.

There are two reasons. First, if you work with employees during the year, in performance planning and communication, they'll understand more fully that the appraisal process isn't something you are going to do to them. They'll understand it as a partnership. That helps create a collaborative climate for the annual meeting. Second, and perhaps more important, there will be no surprises at the appraisal meeting. Since you talk regularly with staff throughout the year, they should know exactly where they stand before the appraisal meeting. You and your employees will already have talked about almost everything that the appraisal meeting will cover. So, if you're doing all of the steps in performance management, the performance appraisal meeting is a review or a summation of the discussions you've had during the year.

Once employees realize that's how it works (and it may take a year or two), they can enter into the process with much lower anxiety levels. That means they'll be less defensive and more open. That makes your role much easier, because you can shift from the "manager as appraiser" to "manager as assistant in employee self-evaluation."

So, let's get focused. What are the characteristics of a performance appraisal meeting that make the process valuable? Performance appraisal meetings succeed under the following conditions:

> **No Surprises**
>
> If I had to choose two words to guide managers in the performance appraisal process, it would be "no surprises." Rarely is there a need to discuss things at the appraisal meeting that haven't been discussed during the year. Once employees realize you're not going to spring surprises on them in the appraisal meeting, they start to work with you and feel more comfortable. If there are surprises, something has gone wrong.

Smart Managing

- The manager takes on the role of helper and problem solver, rather than primary evaluator.
- The employee is actively involved in the partnership and engaged in realistic self-evaluation.
- The manager uses appropriate interpersonal skills to involve the employee.
- The employee understands what to expect, in terms of content and process, before walking in the door.
- The manager treats the meeting as important, something that should not be delayed or rescheduled.
- Both parties understand the why of performance appraisal—that it's not to punish, but to improve performance so everyone wins.

Let's get more specific. We're going to talk about how to prepare yourself and employees for productive performance appraisal meetings. Then we'll discuss the actual meeting. Finally we'll talk about what happens after the meeting.

Preparing and Scheduling

Proper preparation and scheduling are crucial. You need to prepare and schedule so that employees understand what to expect and know that the process is important.

Scheduling

Since performance appraisal leads into the next performance planning cycle, it's ideal to scheduling the appraisals around the end of the fiscal year and/or around the time that the company and work units are developing their goals and objectives for the next year. You are in the best position to decide when they should be done. Some managers and companies conduct the appraisal meetings on or around the employee's hiring anniversary date. The advantage is that this staggers the meetings, so managers aren't doing performance appraisals for all staff during a short period. The disadvantage is that it's harder to link individual objectives to the performance planning process for the next year.

How much time should you allocate to each meeting? That depends. If you've been communicating with your staff during the year about their performance, you don't need as much for the appraisal. It's reasonable to schedule at least an hour of uninterrupted time for the main meeting. If you finish earlier, that's fine. If you go more than several hours, you're probably going to have a fatigue problem. Better to have two shorter meetings than one really long one, since as fatigue sets in people tend to become inattentive and frustrated.

Managers often bump scheduled appraisal meetings when other, "more important" things come up. Bad idea. This sends the message that you're not serious about the process, that it's not a high priority. Schedule it and stick to the schedule. Also, as we suggested with respect to performance planning, arrange not to be interrupted. Have your phone calls held. This is the employee's time. Make it quality time.

Preparing Employees

How can you help staff get ready for the meetings? First, they need to understand the purpose of the meetings and what's going to occur. They also need to know what they should do (if anything) to prepare for the meeting.

> **Making Appointments** Smart Managing
>
> When making appointments to meet with employees, try to schedule them at least two weeks in advance. This gives the employee ample time to prepare for the meeting.

It's hard to overcommunicate with staff on these issues. Here's a pattern you can follow. About a month before you start the appraisal process, meet with all your staff as a group. The meeting can be as short as fifteen minutes. At that meeting, explain that you'll be scheduling meetings with them to review performance. Explain that the reviews are part of the process to improve performance. Explain what's going to happen, and outline anything they need to do to prepare. Invite them to ask any questions or express any concerns they may have.

Then, when scheduling the meetings, we suggest doing it in person with each employee. When you schedule, again review what's going to happen and make sure the employee understands anything he or she might need to do in advance.

Finally, consider sending out to every employee a one-page informal summary memo that reiterates the process. It might be best to send it a day or two before the scheduled meeting, as a

> **Points for Focusing Employees** TRICKS OF THE TRADE
>
> At the staff meeting, in individual discussions, and in any written material, here are some key points to reiterate:
>
> The review process is a partnership. There will be no surprises, since they all know where they stand. It's a problem-solving process. You're going to ask them to evaluate themselves as much as possible. They are in the best position to figure out how they can do their jobs better. It's about looking forward, not looking backward. It's not about blaming.

How Can Employees Prepare?

Smart Managing

Some managers ask employees to do a self-evaluation before the meeting, so manager and employee can compare it with the manager's perceptions. Employees can (and should) review the performance plan for the year. You can suggest that they collect and bring any data or information that might help the two of you identify, explain, and resolve any problems or issues.

reminder of your appointment as well as of what you plan to accomplish.

Preparing Yourself

What do you need to do to prepare yourself for the appraisal meeting? First, make sure you have any documents, data, or information relevant to appraisal discussions. Normally, that would include the employee's performance plan for the year, plus any notes or information from ongoing performance communication during the year. It could also include letters of commendation or complaint from customers or notes regarding phone calls related to the employee's job performance (again, both positive and negative).

Then, just before each appraisal meeting, we recommend taking some time to do two things:

- Remind yourself of your focus—to improve performance. You may want to quickly review the six points we presented earlier in the chapter outlining what makes performance appraisal succeed.
- Review the employee's performance planning document to refresh your memory. You might also think about how you'd evaluate him or her on each of the items—especially if you've asked employees to do self-evaluations.

The Appraisal Meeting

What you do in the appraisal meeting depends in part on whether you're using an objective- or a standards-based approach (as we've suggested) or a rating or ranking form your company insists you complete. It will also depend on whether you've asked employees do a self-evaluation in advance. Here's a brief outline of the steps, if employees have not evaluated themselves in preparation.

- Set the climate and focus
- Use the performance plan or the rating form to evaluate
- Begin performance diagnosis
- Plan for the future
- Document the conversation

Setting the Climate and Focus

As we suggested with respect to performance planning, the first few minutes of the meeting should be allocated to establishing some level of comfort for both parties and focusing (once again) on what will happen and how the meeting will be conducted.

Why, you might ask, should you do this at the performance planning meeting, a month before the appraisal meeting, in writing, when you set the appointment, and once again at the beginning of the appraisal meeting? While that may seem like overkill, keep in mind that most employees have had unpleasant experiences with performance appraisals and feel anxious about them. They also carry some other "baggage" and will tend to see appraisals as a "me vs. you" situation. To overcome those negative forces, you have to keep sending the message about what the meeting is for and make sure your behavior during the meeting is consistent with the goals and process you've set out. After staff have gone through the process with you a few times, you'll have less need to set the climate and focus.

Using the Performance Plan or the Rating Form to Evaluate

Reviewing performance is relatively straightforward, provided you have a clear set of objectives and standards (the performance plan) and communication has been ongoing throughout the year. You go through each of the objectives and standards and determine the degree of success the employee has achieved toward that objective or standard.

We suggest using questions to begin the process. For example: "Tom, let's look at objective X, which was your highest priority for the year. I'd like to know two things: One, whether you feel you've hit the target or not and two, how you know whether you have or not. So, what do you think?" The idea here is to encourage the employee to evaluate himself or herself and to refer to data, information, and so on to justify the assessment. Of course, you may comment on whether or not you agree with the assessment. You'll also need to substantiate your opinion (either positive or negative) with data, information, or observations. If there are significant differences in opinion, try to find some middle ground where you both feel comfortable. If

---

TRICKS OF THE TRADE

Two Good Icebreakers
One way of getting people talking is to start with how they're feeling about the process about to take place. For example: "Tom, usually employees feel a little nervous about these meetings. How are you feeling right now?" That gives you a chance to reassure the anxious employee. Another way is to begin by telling the employee how you feel: "I always worry that these meetings are going to be difficult. I try to remind myself that we've done all our homework, so there won't be any surprises."

---

that's impossible, both you and the employee will need to document your positions. (See "Documenting the Conversation" later in this chapter.) If you did your performance planning well and communicated well throughout the year, you'll find that serious disagreements about performance are unlikely.

What if you have to use a rating system provided by your company? Let's say you have a set of thirty items and you have to assign a rating of 1 (poor) to 5 (excellent) for each of them. How do you get the best out of a bad system?

Here's the trick. You add a step up front. You start the process by operationalizing each item. This means coming to some agreement with the employee about what the item means before talking about the actual rating numbers.

You might say, for example, "John, the first item is 'contributes to obtaining team results.' How would we know or determine whether you've been really lousy at that or really superb? What does that item mean to you?" Or you could say, "John, if someone had been watching you work, how would that person determine how much you contributed to obtaining team results?"

After you have some answers, you get the chance to explain what you think the item means and then you work to ob-

> **When You Disagree**
>
> **Smart Managing**
>
> Ratings are subjective and vague at best. Be flexible about minor differences. Arguing for half an hour about whether a person should get a 3 or a 4 on an item is a waste of time and can poison the process and the relationship.
>
> Obviously if you feel performance is abysmal and the employee thinks it's wonderful, you should talk about the difference. But the ratings themselves aren't going to cause employees to improve. The real value is in the discussion that the ratings generate. (See Chapter 14 for some specific tips on handling disagreement and frustration.)

tain agreement. Once you've established a common understanding of the item, then you can move on to the rating process. Ask the employee to rate himself or herself on the item. Then offer your assessment. If there's a difference, talk about it. Negotiate to find common ground.

Beginning Performance Diagnosis

Determining the extent to which the employee has achieved the objectives or rating his or her performance is probably the most trivial and unimportant part of the appraisal process. The guts of the process—the part that will contribute to better performance in the future—is the diagnosis. Generally this process starts during the appraisal meeting.

The purpose is simple. When the employee has failed to achieve an objective or meet a standard or a rating not very high, you and the employee focus on the reasons. Since Chapter 10 outlines the process of diagnosing performance, we won't go into great detail here. For the moment, here are the key questions to discuss:

- What factors or barriers did you face that might have caused you to miss on this objective or rating item?
- What could you (and I) have done differently so that this objective or standard could have been achieved?
- Is there anything you would have done differently?

The emphasis is on finding causes, identifying barriers, and generating solutions. The focus is on learning, not blaming. That's how you should handle performance problems.

But you should also discuss the positives. When the employee has achieved an objective and met a standard or rated high, determine how he or she did it. Perhaps it was by working harder or bringing in appropriate resources. It's important for staff to know what they need to continue to do to achieve success. So, diagnosis isn't just diagnosing "sickness" but figuring out why "the patient is so darn healthy"!

A final point on diagnosis as part of the appraisal meeting. It's good to start this kind of analysis, but you may not be able to finish it during the meeting. That's OK. You can continue the process of diagnosis during follow-ups, as well as during the next round of performance planning.

Planning for the Future

Action planning is really an extension of the diagnostic process. If you've identified barriers that hurt performance during the last year, then you may want to identify actions that will keep the problems from recurring.

You and the employee may come to some agreements about what either or both of you can do. Your action plans might include arranging

---

TRICKS OF THE TRADE

Recognizing the Positive

It's easy for managers and employees to focus only on the targets missed, rather than also on the targets hit. Strive for a balance. Be particularly alert to situations where the employee has exceeded the standards set or performed extraordinarily well. If you focus on achievements and resolving difficulties, you remove a lot of stress from the situation.

for training or coaching, reallocation of resources, and so on. Obviously what you decide to do depends on what's gone wrong and why. In some cases, the actions required may include what we normally call "disciplinary action." (See Chapter 11.)

Documenting the Conversation

Now, you've pretty much worked through the meeting process. The only remaining step is to document your discussions and the appraisal.

If you're using an objective-based system, the documentation might include the performance plan (objectives and standards), plus some means of indicating whether or not the employee achieved the objectives and met the standards. You may want to add additional notes about the conversation. Where there is significant disagreement, you will want to make note of that and invite the employee to add comments explaining his or her position.

If you're using a rating form, then clearly that will constitute a major part of the documentation. However, it's our opinion that explanatory notes should accompany all completed rating forms, documenting any disagreements or very good or very poor ratings.

Since most companies keep the documentation from appraisal meetings as part of the permanent personnel files, it's essential that both manager and employee sign the documentation. The signatures don't necessarily mean that both parties agree with everything in the appraisal or the documentation. They're just proof that manager and employee had the discussion as documented.

Arrange Any Follow-Ups

Sometimes it's not possible to complete the process in one meeting. Sometimes it makes sense to follow up on a few things, particularly if there are loose ends. For example, you and the employee might need additional information or data to determine whether he or she has achieved an objective. If so, arrange a follow-up meeting, once the data is available. Or, you might want to allow a few days for both you and the employee to consider or reconsider a position or assessment. Sometimes, particularly where there is strong disagreement, this can be an effective technique to enable you to come to an agreement.

Once you've completed the appraisal process, it may be a good time to schedule the performance planning meeting for the new year. It's always a good idea to do the performance appraisal for last year and the performance planning for next year as close together in time as possible. That's because you can use the information from the performance appraisal to work further on preventing problems in the next year.

Manager's Checklist for Chapter 9

❑ Have you done effective performance planning and then communicated about performance throughout the year? If so, the performance appraisal meeting is simply a review of what's gone on during the past year, so there won't be any surprises.

❑ Don't skimp on the preparation. It is absolutely crucial that employees understand the purpose of the appraisal meetings and how they will be conducted. It's also important you remain focused on your purpose.

❑ Any appraisal will be subjective to some degree, particularly where rating scales are used. That means your assessment isn't perfect. An employee's self-assessment won't be perfect. Don't overcommit to a position, particularly if the difference between your assessment and the employee's self-assessment is minimal.

❑ It isn't the rating or the actual assessment that improves performance. What matters is the discussion between you and the employee.

Performance Diagnosis and Improvement: The Key to Success

We don't manage performance for fun. We don't manage performance to get the goods on employees. We don't manage performance to cover our behinds. (Well, sometimes!) The real reason we manage performance is to improve productivity and effectiveness, however you want to define that, and to engineer success for each and every employee.

Let's imagine that you've discussed and planned your employees' performances. They all understand what their jobs involve and how well they need to perform. You meet regularly to communicate about performance, so you have the information you need and employees have what they need. And, you conduct your yearly performance appraisal to identify what each employee has done well and what was done not so well.

What have you accomplished? Not much. You need to aim your efforts not only at clarifying communication, not only at evaluating performance, and not only at providing feedback. The real payoff comes from identifying why performance succeeds when it succeeds and why performance fails when it fails, and then figuring out how to do more of the right stuff and less of the wrong stuff. That's the real key to ongoing success for your company, you, and your employees.

Performance diagnosis is the process we use with an employee to determine the causes of his or her success and/or the causes of his or her difficulties. It can and should occur at any or all stages of the performance management process and in partnership with the employee. Its purpose is to uncover causes so that they can be eliminated and/or overcome.

> **Performance diagnosis** The process we use with an employee to uncover the real causes of his or her success and/or the causes of his or her difficulties. Its purpose is to identify causes of problems so they can be eliminated or overcome. It is done at any time during the year and in partnership with the employee.

Before we discuss performance diagnosis and problem solving, we need to address a fundamental issue: what causes successful performance and what causes less than successful performance?

Causes of Success and "Less than Success"

There are two general approaches to considering the factors that affect the productivity of any individual.

One way of looking at it, and probably the one more familiar to you, involves individual factors. For example, we tend to believe that an individual who is well-trained, smart, motivated, skilled, etc., will be a good performer. You can probably point to your most productive employee and attribute his or her success to a number of individual characteristics. Try it. Describe your most productive employee. What do you think "causes" him or her to succeed?

The second way of thinking about causes of success and failure to achieve goals is more unusual. Although we once believed that each employee controlled his or her own destiny or success, the work of people like W. Edwards Deming has taught us that individual factors aren't the whole story. They may not even be most of the story.

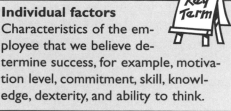

Individual factors Characteristics of the employee that we believe determine success, for example, motivation level, commitment, skill, knowledge, dexterity, and ability to think.

We must also consider the system in which people work. When we talk about this "system," we're referring to things beyond the employee's control. For example, the flow along an assembly line can be logical and effective or illogical and slow down production. Some companies will set up such bureaucratic processes that they cripple individual initiative. Perhaps the proper tools or equipment aren't available to the employee. In the worst cases, you can put a top-notch employee in a really poor system and he or she will perform poorly. In other words, the system, the way work is done, can make it look as if employees are incompetent or unproductive, when the problems are really in the system.

Why is this distinction between individual factors and system factors so absolutely critical?

Most of us attribute success or failure to individual factors first. We search for the employee's flaws first. It's part of our individualistic culture and thinking. The problem is that we don't recognize that performance isn't under the control of each individual, but depends on the individual working within a system. So, what's the outcome? Employee Jack is underperforming. The initial reaction is to send Jack for training or to try to "motivate" or pressure Jack. But what if Jack can't perform his job better, not because of any personal flaw, but because he doesn't have the proper tools? Well, we've wasted time looking in the wrong place for the wrong causes, and wasted money addressing causes that aren't real. Plus, if we blame Jack for a problem beyond his control, we can lose him as a

System factors Causes of success and failure that are beyond the control of individual employees. Examples include poor workflow, excessive bureaucracy, poor communication, and inadequate tools and equipment.

potentially productive employee. Jack doesn't need motivating, or training, or a kick in the behind. If we expect him to pound nails, he needs a hammer, not a screwdriver. Blaming him won't help. We can help only if we identify his need and provide a hammer.

Let me give you another example of factors that can undermine an employee's productivity. One company had a receptionist who was hired to answer phones and to do the office meeting and greeting. She did the job well.

> **⚠ CAUTION!**
> **Error!**
> Probably the most common and destructive management error in performance management is to explain poor performance by first looking for flaws in the individual. Better to start with the possibility that the system may be a primary cause of the problem. If it's not, then move on to individual factors.

After she'd been there a year or so, the organization decided to publish a regular newsletter. Since the receptionist, Sherrie, had a knack for graphic design, the manager agreed to give her the opportunity to develop some desktop publishing skills through training, so she could eventually take on the entire layout task. The idea was that this would enrich her job and make it more interesting and varied. So, she learned how to use a particular desktop publishing program and was eager to begin.

Unfortunately, the company hadn't thought to buy a copy of this program for Sherrie to use. Weeks went by. Months went by. By then another staff member had started producing the newsletter, but nobody talked to Sherrie about it. She stewed and she wondered. She felt cheated, deceived. Guess what happened to her job performance over the next year? She was angry and became cynical and sullen. Because of the stress of her reactions, she took a lot of sick leave. The sad ending to the story? Eventually her performance became a liability and she was laid off.

This is an unfortunate but true story. The environment in which Sherrie worked (including what we have to consider as incompetent management) created the problem. Sherrie didn't create it. But she was eventually blamed for it and punished for it. The whole episode cost the company tens of thousands of dollars in productivity. Was Sherrie blameless? No, probably not. But the issue here is that the management staff should have recognized that their behavior was likely to create a problem and tried to resolve it by communicating better, reshuffling job tasks, or doing whatever was necessary.

The Performance Diagnosis/Improvement Steps

Performance diagnosis is both a problem-solving process (a logical one) and a human process (one that requires teamwork). In this section, we'll map out a general pattern you can use to diagnose performance deficits or problems when they occur. We'll look at the following steps:
- Become aware of a performance gap.
- Identify the nature of the gap and its seriousness.
- Identify possible causes of the gap, both system-related and employee-related.
- Develop an action plan to address the cause of the gap.
- Implement the action plan.
- Evaluate whether the problem has been solved.
- Start over, if necessary.

Becoming Aware of a Performance Gap

The first step in diagnosis and improvement is to recognize that there may be a problem. How does this happen?

There is a mistaken idea that the only way performance gaps or deficits are identified is during the yearly performance appraisal meetings. That's dangerous thinking. If you have a serious problem, do you want to wait as long as a year before knowing? Of course not. Yes, performance appraisal time provides an opportunity to identify problems. But we need to become aware of problems much earlier. So, how else do problems get identified? Let's look at three ways.

First, you can identify problems through the data and information you collect continuously about the important functions of your business. If you're in the customer service industry, perhaps you're monitoring customer satisfaction. That data will help you identify potential problems. If you're in manufacturing, you're probably gathering information about the quantity and quality of products. But data is valuable only if somebody uses it. You'd be amazed at the kinds of data companies collect and never use. So data gathered throughout the year can help you determine whether there's something happening that you should examine more closely.

Second, you can identify problems through your employees. You're communicating with them regularly, right? That's a key element in identifying problems: if problems occur, the employees doing the work will know about them way before anyone else does. Of course, they may not let you know unless they can trust you not to punish them for the problems, even when they may be implicated in the cause. They need to know your focus will be on problem solving, not blaming.

What Data Do You Need?

Some companies and managers don't collect any data and information at all. Others try to collect everything under the sun. Decide what you need to be able to identify potential problems early, and then make sure that information is collected and used.

A final way of identifying problems—in addition to the performance appraisal process, systematic methods of gathering data, and communication from employees—just paying attention. If you get out of your office, it's amazing what you can find out. Are customers smiling? If not, maybe there's a problem. What's the atmosphere in the office? Tense? Relaxed? The old "management-by-walking-around" approach can help you considerably in becoming aware of problems.

Identifying the Nature of the Gap and Its Seriousness

So, you've become aware of a possible performance gap. To fix this problem, you need more information. You need to know several things.

First, it helps to define the problem as precisely as possible. Where does it occur? Under what conditions? How often? Is it occurring with one staff member or are several involved? And of course, how do you know it exists? How does it manifest itself?

Second, you need to determine the seriousness of the problem. Not all performance problems are serious enough to require intervention. The question to ask is, "How does this gap affect or interfere with our ability to achieve our unit and company goals?" Does it cost money because of waste or inefficiency? Are we losing customers because of it? Perhaps it's an internal problem in a team that creates interpersonal friction. Consider two things:

> **Pay Attention!**
>
> Use formal ways of identifying problems or performance gaps (appraisals, data gathering, and communication), but don't rely on them exclusively. Get out of your office and observe what's going on. Listen to people at coffee breaks. Often that's where early difficulties get discussed first.
>
> *Smart Managing*

- The cost of doing nothing.
- The cost of intervening and the savings that will result if you close the performance gap.

If you determine that the problem is not serious enough or costly enough to warrant action, you may choose to monitor it in case it becomes a larger problem. If you decide that the problem is serious enough to address, the next step is to look for possible causes.

Identifying Possible Causes

Look first for problems with the system—the way work is structured, jobs are arranged, tools are available (or not)—before looking for individual causes. There are two points to keep in mind.

> **Look to the Future, Too**
>
> When evaluating the seriousness of a performance gap, consider the effect it has now, of course, but also how it might affect things down the road. Keep small problems and gaps from growing.
>
> *Smart Managing*

First, even problems that, on the surface, seem a result of flaws in an individual may be caused by the system. For example, imagine two staff members in constant conflict, hurting general morale and reducing productivity. Perhaps one or both have "a bad attitude" or lack good communication skills, or perhaps their jobs are ill-defined and it isn't clear who has responsibility for what. It could be that the conflict results from a lack of understanding of the jobs, because the boundaries overlap. That's a system-based cause.

Here's the second point. Don't assume that a performance gap is caused by individual factors just because it occurs with just one person doing the job, and not with other people doing the same job. This may sound strange to you. Doesn't it make sense that, if a problem were caused by poor tools or job structure, it would affect everyone equally? No. That's incorrect. It's possible for person A to succeed in spite of poor tools while person B fails as a result of the same poor tools. If you identify the true or root cause reducing person B's effectiveness, you may find that both person A and person B improve.

Diagnostic Tools and Questions

Determining what's causing a performance gap isn't easy. There are a number of techniques and tools you can use,

> ### The Deceptive Word Processing Problem
> Joanne and Mark did the same job—using a word processor to send letters to customers. The manager noticed that Mark produced about half the number of letters, with a much higher error rate than Joanne. Instead of assuming it was a problem with Mark, the manager looked first for system causes.
>
> It turned out the word processing software was so primitive it didn't have a proper spell checker. Joanne was a good speller; Mark wasn't, so he had to consult a dictionary, which slowed him down. Which is the better solution? Make Mark a better speller? Or find a better, more useful software package? The manager chose to upgrade the word processor—and both Joanne and Mark became more productive!

some statistical and some logical. Since our focus is on the people part of performance management, we'll mention a few simple approaches to use with an employee or by yourself to examine a performance gap.

You can use brainstorming to generate ideas about possible causes. Brainstorming is a technique involving two or more people to generate as many ideas as possible in a short time. Usually a question is presented and participants generate possible answers in a rapid-fire format. The key to brainstorming is to avoid evaluating ideas as they're presented. Just write them down. When the ideas stop, you go back and sift through the possibilities to see which ideas make sense.

A second method is called the "Five Whys" technique. Its purpose is to explore beneath the surface. You can use the technique by yourself, with an employee in private, or in a group problem-solving process.

Here's how it works. Define a "why?" question. For example, "Why does Mark produce fewer letters and make more spelling errors?" Answer it. Mark is less productive because he's looking up words in the dictionary. Don't stop there. Ask the next "why?" question: "Why is he looking up words in the dictionary?" You might have several possible answers for this. Pursue the one that gets you to another "why?" question. Two possible answers: "Mark is stupid" (uh-oh...that's not a productive path, is it?) or "The spell checker in the word processing program is poor." Next "why?" question: "Why (or in what way) is the spell

> **Two-Person Brainstorming**
>
> John, a manager, and his employee, Fred, were looking at possible causes of a drop in Fred's output over the last four months. In dialogue, they determined the details of the problem (when it occurred, how often, and under what conditions). Then John suggested brainstorming: "Fred, let's see how many possible causes of this problem we can come up with. We'll just blurt them out, make a quick note, and not discuss them. Then we'll go back and see what makes sense."

checker poor?" Possible answers: "It's old" or "It uses a Swahili dictionary and we write letters only in English." Ask "why?" again: "Why is it old?"

You continue this process until you get a nonsensical answer or it's clear that continuing to ask "why?" isn't going to get you any further. Try to ask it five times.

Brainstorming and the Five Whys technique will help you improve your diagnosis of performance gaps. It's important to ask the right questions—of yourself and of the employee. Here are some to consider:

- Is the gap a result of the employee not being clear about expectations, standards, or authority levels?
- Does the employee have a good record? Is problem a recent occurrence?
- Is the gap a result of a skill deficit, something training could address?
- Could the employee do the task if his or her life depended on it? (If no, then it's a skill deficit. If yes, it points to a psychological or attitudinal problem.)
- Is the employee capable of learning the needed skills?
- What remedial steps have been taken in the past?

The Remaining Steps

Once we believe we've identified a cause or causes, we need to develop an action plan to address the issue. That's a fairly straightforward process, preferably done in partnership with the employee. After you've formalized the plan, which you may want to document on paper, you need to implement it. So, for example, if you and the employee believe the performance gap is a result of a lack of skill in a specific area, you might arrange for ongoing coaching, partnering, or training. If it's due to some psychological problem, you might refer to an employee assistance program or counseling program.

Then, after putting your plan into action, you need to determine if the gap still exists. If so, then perhaps you need to examine how you implemented the solution. Or maybe you misidentified the cause. If that's the case, then you go back to the beginning to diagnose the problem again.

Treat your conclusions about possible causes and possible solutions as hypotheses. Allow for the possibility that your diagnosis could be incorrect. So you do your best, and then, if that doesn't work, you try something else.

The People Process

Whether you apply the simple problem-solving and diagnostic approaches we've discussed or you use more complex statistical techniques, the results will depend on how you handle the process. Diagnosing problems requires the cooperation of those involved, and people won't cooperate with you unless you use appropriate people and focusing skills. To help you, we've compiled a list of principles and tips.

- Diagnosis works best when manager and employee are working together in the problem-solving process. As a manager you need the information the employee has about the problem. The employee may not see the whole picture and can benefit from your knowledge and understanding. Aim to create a nonblaming environment.
- There's a significant difference between *blaming* and *diagnosing*. Don't dwell on the past and make accusations. Diagnosis is about preventing and fixing problems. In any discussions about performance gaps, make it clear that your goal is to help the employee fix or prevent the problem. Make it really clear.
- Consider timing. Diagnosing problems is least effective when the people involved are upset, angry, or frustrated. Before broaching a performance gap issue with an employee, ask yourself, "Am I able to discuss this constructively at this point? Or am I frustrated enough to mishandle it or sound like I'm blaming?"
- This approach to diagnosis can be effective in teams. If you observe that a team member is having a problem,

present the issue to the group as a system issue. That means you're going to focus not on the person with the difficulty, but on the entire process. So, rather than asking, "How can we help Sam type better?" ask, "How can we work together to improve the process we use to get letters out so it's easier or faster?"

- If you believe the cause of a performance gap or problem rests with the individual, it's best to start the diagnosis process in private. Never do anything in public that might embarrass an employee.

Manager's Checklist for Chapter 10

❏ Treat the performance diagnosis process as a cycle. Use the information you have to determine the cause of the problem. Work in partnership with the employee. Keep in mind that you could be wrong. If the remedial action does not work, start the process again.

❏ It's almost impossible to solve performance problems on your own. And management power very rarely can force someone to perform better. Approach the problem in partnership with the employee. After all, if you can solve it, everyone benefits.

❏ Look first at possible system causes, and then at possible employee causes. Many problems have multiple causes: the system and the employee interact in ways that cause the problem.

❏ If the performance problem is worth addressing, it's probably also worth documenting. That means keep a written record of your communication with the employee and the steps you've taken together to solve the problem.

Performance Management and Discipline

John anticipated a rough day at the office. As he dressed for work, he tried to figure out how to handle today's performance review with Brian. In the last year, Brian's performance had been really below par and had even attracted the attention of the executives upstairs. Just yesterday, the vice president had called John in to talk about it and made it clear she expected him to do something fast. "Give him a month to shape up, John," she'd said, "and if he doesn't improve, then out he goes. You have to take some disciplinary action here."

On the way to work, John couldn't get the meeting out of his mind. John thought to himself, "Gee, I've kept quiet about this, hoping his performance would shape up. Now what a mess... two customers lost just this week. What the heck am I going to do? I hate this job!"

You probably understand the feeling of dread John was experiencing. Disciplining employees is one of the most trying and stressful things managers do. But it's a responsibility of management. The question is, "How do we use performance management for disciplinary action so that it's likely to produce a positive outcome? That's the question we're going to address in this chapter. Before you read on, consider the following questions about John's situation.

- Given the information you have about the situation, is it likely the meeting will go well and be productive?
- Are John and the vice president looking at discipline in a way that's likely to succeed?
- What things should have happened over the last year to prevent this situation?
- Is the vice president's "order" in the best interests of the company, John, or Brian?
- What pieces are missing?

The Meaning of Discipline

What does "discipline" mean? If you look in a dictionary, you will find not one, not two definitions, but many definitions. At one end of the spectrum, discipline means forcing another person to be obedient. That's a common meaning. For many people, the word conjures up some harsh images, images of punishment, retribution, and even pain. At the other end of the spectrum, "discipline" refers to helping people through teaching and training. For example, a disciple is someone who follows the teachings of another.

Which definition is being applied in your organization? If it's a typical company, you will find that most people understand discipline as it relates to obedience, rather than teaching. Is that the best way to look at discipline? Or is it better to think of discipline as teaching?

The answer to both questions is no. Forcing obedience doesn't usually work. On the other side, while discipline as teaching is a nice notion, the reality is that managers have a responsibility to act when teaching and helping fail. Sooner or later, performance problem situations must be resolved. Sometimes that requires unilateral action by a manager.

We need some way of looking at discipline that doesn't encourage managers to "use the whip" but addresses the real responsibility managers have for solving workplace problems. What might that definition look like?

Discipline is the process used to address performance problems; it involves the manager in identifying and communicating performance problems to employees, and in identifying, communicating, and applying consequences if the performance problems are not remedied. In its early stages, it resembles or is even identical to the process of performance management, where problems are identified and manager and employee work together to solve them. However, when working together doesn't solve the problem, then the manager is responsible for addressing the problem with other tools, which may involve unilateral action, maybe the application of "consequences."

Consequences are whatever occurs as a direct result of an action. Managers have a right to impose consequences when an employee is always late and disrupting work. Managers have a right to impose consequences, even job termination, in a number of situations, after exhausting all other avenues. It's more than a right; it's a responsibility.

> **Discipline** The process used to address performance problems; it involves the manager in identifying and communicating performance problems to employees, and in identifying, communicating, and applying consequences if the performance problems are not remedied. In its early stages, it resembles or is even identical to the process of performance management.

It's important to understand the difference between *consequences* and *punishment*. When you punish somebody, it's something you do because you have the power to do it. Often it's an emotional process carried out in anger. When you apply consequences, the other person is choosing, by his or her inappropriate or ineffective behavior, to deal with the consequences of that behavior. The mind-set is different. Punishment is emotional, vengeful. It involves getting even

Smart Managing

Make Sure They Understand

If a consequence is something an employee chooses through his or her actions or inaction, the employee must know in advance that a particular action or behavior will result in a specific consequence. That means it's the manager's responsibility to communicate what consequences will be associated with what employee behavior long before imposing those consequences.

and is parental. Applying consequences is emotionally neutral, not personal, and takes place with the recognition that the other person has chosen the consequence through action or inaction. If you see discipline as punishment, it will almost always be unpleasant and destructive. If you apply consequences, it's less likely to be unpleasant and more likely to produce some constructive results.

Principles of Disciplinary Action

It's your right and responsibility as a manager to apply consequences. But there are some principles that should guide you in taking any disciplinary action.

- Disciplinary action must conform to the laws in your location and any labor agreements in place.
- Any disciplinary action must be documented completely, in detail—actual performance gap, how it was identified, how it was communicated to employee, and steps taken to resolve the problem.
- Disciplinary action should use the least level of force and pressure needed to solve the performance problem.
- The more force brought to bear, the less likely you are to achieve a constructive, long-term, win-win solution. Use strong discipline measures only when absolutely necessary and justified by the seriousness of the problem.
- The more specifically you can describe the performance problem, the more likely you can solve it with the employee—and the more likely you will be protected legally if you need to use strong disciplinary action.

The Purpose of Disciplinary Action/Consequences

Think of the disciplinary process as a problem-solving tool. To use it effectively, you need to know what problems it's meant to address. At a "big level," the purpose of the process is to remedy a performance deficit. In the early stages of the disciplinary process, we work with the employee in question to identify the cause(s) of inadequate job performance and formulate a plan to help the employee improve.

In the very early stages, the discipline process is identical to the overall performance management process. This changes if time passes and performance doesn't improve. When performance diagnosis, coaching, giving feedback, and other techniques don't work, the focus shifts to determining what to do with an employee who is consistently below expectations. In the later stages of the disciplinary process, the manager may be forced to act more unilaterally and less cooperatively.

> **Procrastination—**
> **The Big Mess Maker**
> Probably the most common mistake managers make regarding performance management and discipline is waiting too long to discuss performance deficits. They often let things go because discussing performance problems is uncomfortable. Don't procrastinate: it generally just makes the situation more difficult and more damaging. Deal with problems as they arise.

The Progressive Discipline Steps

Let's define "progressive discipline." It's a process in which the manager uses the least possible pressure and force to solve a performance problem, but applies consequences if more cooperative problem solving doesn't work.

So, you start out gently and supportively. Then, if the problem continues, you use a little more managerial power. At the extreme, progressive discipline may result in terminating the employee, which is the ultimate use of managerial power. However, we always look first for cooperative solutions, working together, since unilateral approaches cause everyone to lose something.

We can divide the progressive discipline steps into three phases. The first phase is identical to the performance management process we have described. The second involves communicating and applying consequences that are mild. The third involves a lot of unilateral management power.

Phase One: Identification and Cooperation

The first phase of the discipline process consists of the following steps:

- Identify the performance problem.
- Communicate about the problem.
- Diagnose the problem.
- Plan actions to eliminate the problem.
- Evaluate the results of the actions.

First, you identify the performance problem. Problems can be identified through regular communication and status meetings, observation, or yearly performance appraisal reviews by comparing actual achievement and the goals and objectives agreed upon during performance planning. The first question: Is there a gap between what the employee is doing and what you need the employee to do? The second question: What is that gap, specifically?

Once a problem or gap is identified, you must communicate it to the employee. In some cases, you and the employee will have worked together to discover the performance gap. In other cases, such as if you observe unacceptable behavior, you must communicate the problem to the employee in a cooperative and problem-solving way.

The next step is to diagnose the problem. Why is it occurring? Is it a result of an employee's lack of skill or knowledge? Is it caused by something not under the employee's control? You determine the cause to ensure that it relates to the employee and to help in the next step, action planning to eliminate the problem.

Now both you and the employee know there's a performance gap and have some tentative ideas about what's causing the problem. At this point you sit down with the employee and work out some possible ways to eliminate the problem. For example, if the cause is not under the employee's control, then the solutions may have to do with changing the way work is done elsewhere. Or, if the cause is a gap in employee skills, understanding, or learning, you may coach him or her or arrange for training or additional learning.

The final step in this first phase is to evaluate the success of the action plan. Has the problem been eliminated? If so, the process ends here. If not, you can go back to the top of the cycle, to determine if your diagnosis might have been incorrect, or you can move on to the second phase of the progressive discipline process.

> **Look for Causes in the System**
>
> As we mentioned in the last chapter, don't assume that the performance is under the control of the individual employee, that he or she is incompetent or unmotivated. Check first to see if the system (how work is allocated, done, etc.) might be causing the problem or at least be a contributing factor.

Phase Two: Cooperative Consequences

If, after several cycles of identifying causes and trying solutions, the problem continues, it may be time for you to communicate the consequences that will occur if performance does not improve. This phase consists of the following steps:

- Identify reasonable consequences.
- Communicate the consequences.
- Monitor performance for improvement.
- Apply the consequences.
- Evaluate the results of the consequences.

At this point the ideal situation is for the manager to work with the employee to identify reasonable consequences. A reasonable consequence is something that is in proportion to the performance problem and is seen as a logical and non-punitive consequence.

Imagine an employee is chronically late for work. A reasonable consequence might be that the employee is required to make up any missing time or have his or her paycheck docked for the time missed. This would be a logical consequence because it's directly related to the problem of tardiness. An unreasonable consequence would be to have the employee clean out the lavatories for a week. This punishment would be seen as mean and nasty and would make the situation worse because it's not related to the problem behavior.

After you've identified consequences, make sure the employee understands them. If you involve the employee in setting the consequences, then he or she understands them. If you decide on the consequences unilaterally, it's critical to communicate them to the employee. In either situation, it's a good idea to document the discussion so there's evidence that you've discussed the issue. It's also useful to schedule a meeting to assess whether performance has improved.

Between the notification of consequences and the assessment meeting, both manager and employee should be monitoring the performance problem. If you're going to apply the consequences, you'll need some evidence that the problem still exists.

Smart Managing

Identify Consequences with Employee

It's much better if the employee identifies the consequences or at least agrees to them. This isn't always possible, of course. But it's worth a try.

Start by inviting the employee to share in establishing fair consequences: "We must find a way to solve this problem. I need to figure out what to do if you continue to be late. What do you think would be a fair consequence if you're late again?" If that doesn't work, state your consequence and ask: "I think that's a fair way to handle this, if you're late again. Do you feel that's fair?"

At the assessment meeting, you'll review performance. If the problem has been eliminated, the process stops here. If not, then you apply the consequences.

Meet with the employee privately. Be sure that you're feeling calm, in control of your emotions. Indicate that the performance problem still exists and that you need to apply the agreed-upon consequences. Do so unemotionally and offer to help in any way you can.

Finally, schedule another meeting to review the problem and to discuss further consequences if the problem has not been eliminated.

Phase Three: Unilateral Consequences

Our goal is to work with the employee as much as possible to solve problems. After all, if we have to use heavy-handed methods, we're likely to create more problems than we solve. In any event, harsh consequences often result in lose-lose situations. However, what happens if the cooperative steps you've taken fail? You work with the employee to identify problem causes, you provide coaching and training and support, and you use mild consequences to show you're serious about the issue and to encourage improvement—but the problem continues or gets even worse. What then?

Management has a right and an obligation, within the constraints of any labor agreement or laws, to take more serious action to deal with the problem. If it's clear that you can't work with an employee, then you may need to lay out a set of stronger consequences, particularly if the performance problem is severe. Since these consequences are strong, it's unlikely the employee will agree with them, so you will be applying them unilaterally.

The fundamental process for identifying and applying unilateral consequences is the same as we've outlined in previous sections. You still need to identify consequences, communicate them, document your communication, monitor performance to identify whether the problem is solved, and apply consequences as needed.

Disciplinary Process in Action

Let's go back to our example at the beginning of the chapter concerning John, his employee Brian, and the vice president. We asked whether you thought the "disciplinary meeting" between John and Brian would be successful. The answer is, "Not likely." Why?

First, there hasn't been ongoing communication between John and Brian. It sounds like John has avoided dealing with the problem when it was small and is dealing with it now only because his boss is pressuring him. It's going to be difficult to work with Brian under these circumstances.

Second, at this point both John and his boss are looking at discipline as something they're going to do to Brian without having explored other options or even having identified what might be causing the problem. They've let it go too long and painted themselves into a corner.

Smart Managing

Keep Your Boss Informed

Because disciplinary action can create bad feelings, even if done as well as possible, it's a good idea to discuss with your boss what you're doing. There are several reasons. First, he or she should be aware of what's going on. Second, you may get some guidance and support from your boss. Third, you want to make sure that he or she is comfortable with your actions and will support your decisions.

We also asked what should have happened to prevent this situation. John and Brian should have followed the entire performance management process—planning, ongoing communication, diagnosis, and formal review. If that process did not work, then John should have used a progressive discipline approach, first trying to work with Brian. If that failed, then John and Brian should have identified consequences appropriate to the problem, consequences that John should then have applied if necessary. If all of the cooperative steps failed, then John should take unilateral action to solve the problem.

We asked about whether the vice president's order to read the riot act to Brian was in the best interests of the company, John, or Brian. The answer is, "No."

By setting and applying harsh consequences without pursuing other avenues, John and the vice president will place Brian and the company on opposite sides and set up a potential confrontation. If that happens, everyone loses. By not working with him first, John and the vice president may turn Brian into an even worse performance problem. If push comes to shove and John fires Brian, the company loses its investment in Brian and will have to select and hire a replacement—a very costly process.

So, let's see how John, Brian, and his company should have handled this situation.

Getting It Right: A Worst-Case Scenario

Around the beginning of the fiscal year, John and Brian sat down to set some objectives and targets for the new year. Since part of Brian's job was to increase sales, they agreed on what both believed was a realistic sales target. Both John and Brian signed off on the performance planning document.

John set up a regular reporting system: every two months, he would sit down with each employee to gauge progress toward his or her objectives and identify problems. When he met with Brian, it was clear there was a problem. His figures were declining. This was the "early warning system" in action. At that meeting John communicated his concern: "Brian, it's early in the year but it looks like, if things continue, you're not going to hit the targets we set together. I'd like to meet with you to see if we can identify

Working with, Not Against Smart Managing

Notice the focus. John is working with Brian as part of the performance management process. Also, rather than pushing Brian to come up with answers on the spot, he asks Brian to think about it over the next week. Setting the date for the meeting provides a structure for the process. There's no hint at coercion, no threat. It's early.

what we can do together to turn this around. How about next Monday? When we meet, I would like your view on what's causing the drop and what can be done about it."

The Diagnosis Process

At the next meeting, John asked Brian a number of questions intended to identify causes for the performance problem. Brian had a list of possibilities, none of which seemed to suggest he might be responsible for the problem. (That's not atypical in performance problems.) He said, "Well, John, you know you're asking all of us to take on lots of responsibilities here and something has to give. I have lots of paperwork to do and no secretary and it slows me down."

John was annoyed at the response, because he knew that there was more to the story. Several clients had contacted him asking to work with anyone but Brian. While the clients hadn't given reasons for their request, John suspected that Brian might not be treating clients with respect and consideration. So he replied, "Brian, it might be that the paperwork and other job tasks are slowing you down, and we need to look at that to see what can be done. But a few clients have told me that they don't want to work with you anymore. Is it possible that somehow you're turning people off?" Brian replied, "Well, anything's possible but I doubt it."

At this point John decided to give Brian the benefit of the doubt and asked him what he thought could be done. Brian came up with some suggestions that were possible for the short term: some additional help with the paperwork and release from a low-priority project.

John agreed to these suggestions. He then closed the meeting with these comments: "Brian, we need to watch this closely, because we can't get to the end of the year without you reaching your target. So to make sure we understand each other, I'll arrange for the support you want, but we need to meet again in one month to see if that has solved the problem. We need to see some movement in the right direction over the next four weeks. I'll write a short memo, just for the two of us, summarizing this meeting so there isn't any misunderstanding. I'd like it if you would sign a copy for me."

During the next month, John decided to talk with some of the clients to get some details about the problem. Reluctantly, they indicated that Brian seemed slow and disorganized, often got some things wrong, and didn't seem to be helpful. On rare occasions he became snippy with clients. John made some notes for future reference.

The Follow-up Meeting

The first thing John and Brian discussed at the next meeting was whether Brian's suggestions had solved the problem. There was a slight improvement, but it still appeared that Brian was likely to fall way below the standard agreed upon. John decided he needed a firmer approach.

"Brian," he said, "it seems to me that we're not hitting the real problem here. I've talked with customers and it sounds like you may be feeling pressured and coming across as impatient. It also sounds like you might benefit from some help with time management, since there might be ways you can structure your work so you don't feel under so much pressure. What do you think?"

Brian replied somewhat defensively—another sign of a difficult performance problem. Since Brian didn't seem willing to agree freely, John put it another way.

"Brian, I'm willing to wait one more month—if you feel confident that you can get your figures up. If things haven't changed by the end of the month, I'm going to ask you to attend a seminar on time management and another on in-

> **Allow the Employee to Save Face**
>
> Give the employee the benefit of the doubt. Be careful with how you phrase things and the tone you use. Try to view things as positively as possible. Avoid blaming. Always treat the employee with respect: that's most important.

terpersonal communication to see if that's helpful. Meanwhile, I'm going to meet with you every week to talk about some tricks and techniques that might help you."

At the end of the meeting, John again summarized the conversation in a brief memo, which he had Brian sign. It seemed that Brian felt insulted and was resisting the help offered to him.

During the weekly coaching meetings, Brian seemed more and more sullen. John realized that if things didn't improve before the next monthly meeting, he would have to impose more serious consequences.

The Consequences Meeting

After reviewing the figures and finding no improvement, John took the next step. First, he applied the mild consequences that he'd mentioned in the previous meeting and informed Brian of the dates of the training sessions he was to attend. Then he went further.

"Brian," he said, "This is getting to be a serious problem. The six other staff doing jobs like yours are smack on target. We've tried a number of things to get things on track. I'm willing to work with you a bit more and help, but if you don't hit the targets by the end of the year, we have to look at your job classification and salary structure, since you're producing like an entry-level employee rather than a senior salesperson. Or look to see if there's some other job in which you might find a better fit. We'll talk about those options when the time comes. But I want you to know that, one way or another, we need to find a solution. I'll do everything I can to help, but ultimately, what happens is going to be up to you."

Again, John took some notes and put together a memo, which he asked Brian to sign.

Applying Consequences at the Annual Performance Meeting

Despite other meetings during the year, by the time a year had passed and it was time for the performance review, nothing had changed. If anything, Brian's performance and attitude had worsened. Because John had worked with Brian during the year, there were no surprises at the appraisal meeting. They went through the criteria and established that Brian had not hit his targets. The next step was to apply the consequences outlined earlier in the year.

John approached this in the following way: "Brian, I know it's been a tough year for you. We've both worked really hard to get your sales figures up. I think at this point that we need to discuss whether you want to consider taking another position that might be a better fit or whether you would prefer to stay in sales. You should know that, if you stay in sales, we'll have to look at classifying you at a lower level. The good part is that if your sales figures go up to a senior level, we can reclassify you quickly. So, there are some options here, and you might want to take a few days to think about them. I can give you some additional information about other positions."

The Final Outcome

While John did everything possible to help Brian, the outcome wasn't great. After all, this isn't a fairy tale but a situation that happens in most workplaces at some time or other. Brian transferred to another position in the firm and was eventually terminated because he seemed to have developed a negative attitude and wasn't productive.

Did the disciplinary process fail? It depends on how you look at it. The company lost its investment in Brian and, of course, Brian wasn't too pleased with the whole experience. In that sense it didn't work.

In the larger sense, though, it did work. John could sleep easy and without

> **Make It Easy on Yourself**
>
> **TRICKS OF THE TRADE**
>
> If, at every step of the way, you help the employee, support the employee, and work cooperatively with the employee to solve performance problems, it makes it somewhat easier if you have to fire the person. At least you'll know you've acted with integrity and honesty. If you don't try helping first, you may have trouble looking at yourself in the mirror.

guilt, because he knew he'd tried everything possible to salvage the employee. Throughout the process, he acted with honesty and integrity. The company, because it went "by the book," had sufficient documentation to protect itself if Brian chose to file a legal challenge. And, perhaps as important, the problem was eventually solved. Perhaps not in the most desirable way, but solved nonetheless. What problem? The company couldn't support a poor performance over a period of years, but not just for the obvious financial reason. The other sales staff were aware that Brian wasn't productive and expected management to take action. If John had avoided taking that action, he would have allowed the performance problem to adversely affect the entire sales staff and undermine the credibility of management.

Manager's Checklist for Chapter 11

❏ Don't procrastinate when performance problems come to your attention. The earlier you deal with them, the more likely you will be able to do so helpfully and without anger.

❏ Always start with the helping role. If that doesn't work, you can apply consequences and move to more unilateral decision making. Always use the least possible force.

❏ Make sure you've done a proper diagnosis of the reasons for the performance deficit. If it's a result of factors beyond the employee's control (e.g., problems in the system), it isn't fair or useful to take action as if it were the employee's fault.

❏ Any consequences you choose should be appropriate and proportional to the performance problem. Serious problems require serious consequences, while less serious problems require less serious consequences.

Performance Management Variations

So far we've focused on more traditional approaches to performance management and appraisal. We've outlined a system, based on mutually agreed-upon objectives and standards of performance that are then used in the appraisal process. We've also mentioned the common use of ratings systems and the unfortunate use of ranking systems.

People continue to experiment with variations in managing performance, evaluating it, and providing feedback. In this chapter we'll consider four variations. We'll look at two methods that change the way feedback and appraisal information travel: 360-degree evaluation and bidirectional evaluation. The third approach, which we call "Effectiveness Enhancement Systems," is designed to orient performance management toward the needs of its customers, the employees. The final system we call the "using your head no system system."

360-Degree Feedback/Evaluation Techniques

Over the years our understanding of work has changed a bit. Traditional performance management systems focus on the importance of doing what the boss expects you to do. If the boss is the person an employee has to please, then it makes sense that the boss should provide feedback to the employee and evaluate or assess the employee's success. That still makes some sense. But some argue that the boss is not the only person who is important and not the only person who should be assessing the employees. Why not?

Because companies don't succeed or fail based on how pleased the boss might be ... or the vice president or the CEO. Companies succeed when they please the customer, the person who pays. While it's a good idea for employees to receive feedback and be evaluated by the boss, some people suggest that they also hear from the customers. That just makes sense.

There's more. As we mentioned earlier in this book, what each employee does affects others. Shouldn't we capture that interaction and interdependence somehow in performance management and appraisal? After all, what happens if an employee does his or her job well, but interferes with everyone else and keeps them from doing their best? Perhaps employees need feedback and information from their colleagues, so they can improve and become better team members.

So, now we have three potential sources of feedback and information about performance—the manager, customers, and co-workers. There's one other group to consider.

Customers are the people who take what the company produces, the output. But there are also the suppliers, those who provide the input, the materials the company transforms. Experts in customer service and quality improvement suggest that those relationships are also important. So, we have another potential source of information and feedback, at least for employees who deal with suppliers.

A case can be made for using feedback and evaluation information from all these sources.

In an attempt to collect and make use of information from important multiple sources, some companies have started using an approach called 360-degree feedback. That's 360 degrees, as in a circle, the idea being that information and feedback are collected from all sources—from the manager, the customer, co-workers, and suppliers—rather than only from a single source, the manager.

How Does It Work?

Typically 360-degree evaluation information is collected once a year, although it can be solicited throughout the year. Almost all formal 360-degree evaluation techniques use some kind of rating form, as we discussed in Chapter 8. Usually forms are developed to be used by the manager, co-workers, customers, and suppliers.

> **Key Term**
> **360-degree evaluation or appraisal** A method of collecting information, providing feedback, and evaluating performance that relies on multiple sources of information, usually the manager, customers, co-workers, and, if appropriate, suppliers.

Typically, ratings will be collected anonymously, so feedback givers will feel more at ease to rate honestly. The ratings may then be summarized for the employee being rated, either by human beings or by some computer program. Ideally each employee will have an opportunity to discuss the ratings with his or her manager. There are, of course, many variations possible. For example, one company has set up a completely automated touch-tone feedback system available twenty-four hours a day. Other companies use generic rating forms and software to analyze the data.

Advantages of 360-Degree Feedback

The strength of the 360-degree feedback process? It involves more information sources than traditional manager-employee performance management systems do. That means greater potential for identifying problem areas (or employee strengths) than if only the manager and employee are involved.

There's another important advantage as a feedback mechanism. In traditional feedback systems, in which only the manager evaluates, employees can discount the feedback because it comes from just one person, who may be biased, have a personal agenda, or be just plain wrong. In a 360-degree system, if the same kinds of evaluations come from the boss, co-workers, and customers, the information is harder to discount. So, for example, if customers, the manager, and co-workers indicate that Fred may not be using the best communication skills, perhaps Fred may be more able to accept that feedback because it's coming from several sources.

Disadvantages of 360-Degree Feedback

First, there's a logistical issue. The 360-degree feedback process involves much more data and information than with single-source feedback methods. That strength can also be a problem, because collecting and organizing all that data can be costly. And, because there may be a lot of information to summarize, there's a tendency for the process to become mechanical and paper-driven—to move away from direct communication between people to communication by form or printout.

> **⚠ CAUTION!**
> ### Use 360 as Feedback Only
> Most experts agree that using the results of 360-degree appraisals to determine promotions and pay levels can be very risky because of the use of ratings and the issue of how accurate or objective the assessments might be. If you use a 360-degree approach, consider it as a way of providing employees with information about their performance, but not to make any final determination regarding the quality of work.

Perhaps the biggest drawback of 360-degree approaches is that they usually use rating scales. They suffer from the disadvantages of any system based on ratings. The feedback, while potentially valuable, may not be specific enough to help employees know what they need to do to improve. It also may not be objective enough or precise enough to protect companies if they take disciplinary action based on the information collected.

Finally, it isn't always easy to make sense of ratings and information from various sources, because those sources don't always agree. For example, a manager may rate an employee's communication skills as excellent, co-workers may rate them as just average, and customers may rate them as poor. Then what?

The Bottom Line on 360-Degree Feedback

> ### Before Starting 360-Degree Feedback
>
> **Smart Managing**
>
> 360-degree feedback has become a fad, so be careful. Before you decide to go that route, read everything you can find on the process, not just what a salesperson presents to you about the magic technological ways to make it work.
>
> Keep in mind that any approach (even 360-degree) will succeed or fail based on the *people*, not the *technology*. Evaluate carefully what it will cost you and how it will add value by improving performance—if at all.

It's a complicated process. Like any system, 360-degree feedback isn't perfect. The value you get from it will depend not so much on the forms but on how well you can use the information to identify performance strengths and weaknesses and to help employees improve. Ultimately, as with all performance management systems, its success will be determined by the people factor—communicating between people.

Bidirectional Evaluation

Bidirectional evaluation is the fancy term for saying that evaluation and feedback can flow in two directions, not just from the manager to the employee (the traditional way), but also from the employee to the manager. So, the manager evaluates the employee's performance and the employee evaluates the manager. What's the logic here?

It gets down to how we define the manager's job. If we define that job as "helping employees do their jobs," then it makes sense that managers need feedback about that part of their job. Just like everyone else, to better support and improve the performance of their staff, they need to know what

⚠ CAUTION!

If You Can't Stand the Heat...

If you're going to ask employees how you're doing as a manager or how you might help them, first ask yourself, "Can I handle negative comments calmly, fairly, and nondefensively?"

If you're not sure, then don't ask. The worst thing you can do is ask for feedback from staff, and then demean them by arguing about what they tell you.

they should change. If the employees are the manager's "customers," doesn't the manager need to hear from them about what works and doesn't work? Sure. That's the logic.

Bidirectional evaluation can be formalized into performance appraisal meetings. In fact, if employee feedback is considered part of the manager's formal evaluations, it resembles a variation of 360-degree feedback. But, it doesn't have to be a formal, written process. The real strength of bidirectional evaluation is that it can be done informally as well, interwoven into the communication between two people as part of improving everyone's performance. It's simple. Just ask staff how you can support and help them further. If you ask the right questions, and are open to the answers, you can learn a good deal about your management behavior and how you can improve it.

Advantages of Bidirectional Evaluation

Perhaps the most important plus for bidirectional evaluation is the message it sends. It places manager and employee firmly on the same side—provided it's done well, of course. It opens up the traditional one-way performance discussions into a collaboration in which manager and employee can work together so both can improve and everyone benefits. That's an extremely powerful message.

Disadvantages of Bidirectional Evaluation

As an informal process of two-way communication between manager and employee, bidirectional evaluation doesn't have a great number of disadvantages. There may be some cautions, however.

The success of the process will depend on the manager's interpersonal skills—how effective the manager is at asking questions so the employee feels comfortable being honest and open. Some managers lack those skills or have developed ineffective relationships with staff, where trust is minimal. In those situations, employees just won't be straightforward.

Some managers are not prepared to hear what employees might say about them or, more important, are not prepared to act on the information they receive. This is really a problem, since it makes the manager seem insincere or untrustworthy. If you're going to ask employees how you can improve your management performance, you must be prepared to act on the answers you receive.

Bottom Line on Bidirectional Evaluation

The main strength of bidirectional evaluation is that it puts manager and employee on the same side. It's best used to build a spirit of working together and as informal communication. It needn't be formalized or written down, although you can do that if you wish.

Effectiveness Enhancement Systems

"Effective Enhancement Systems" is the term that Bacal & Associates uses to refer to a way to manage performance that:

- is individualized to meet the needs of each employee or each work unit
- considers each individual employee as the "customer" or consumer of performance management
- is aimed at improving performance by giving each employee what he or she needs to improve (primarily feedback the way the employee wants and needs it)

One of the problems with most performance management systems as implemented is that they rely on a "one size fits all" model. That is, whatever system is used, there's an expectation that every employee in the organization will take part in

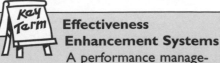

Effectiveness Enhancement Systems
A performance management approach that involves manager and each employee in working together to determine the details of how performance should be managed—the forms, the methods, the frequency of meetings, etc. It places the individual employee in the position of the consumer of the process.

the same process, use the same forms, and have similar information recorded. In other words, it's an attempt to standardize the approach, whether it be using performance objectives, ratings, rankings, or even 360-degree feedback.

Here are some questions we need to ask:

- If our aim is to help individuals perform better, are we comfortable with the idea that everyone will benefit by using the same techniques for providing feedback, evaluating performance, and communication, and by using the same forms?
- Is it possible that one employee might benefit from having some clear objectives but another might improve more effectively with some form of simple rating system?
- Could it be we have to meet more frequently with some people than others?
- Finally, if the goal is to improve performance, can we treat each person as an individual with different needs? Does it make sense to *individualize* the process?

Perhaps it makes sense to involve each employee in determining how performance will be planned and evaluated—like treating the employee as the customer. Why? Because in a sense the employee is the consumer of the process. If the process doesn't give the employee what he or she needs and wants to perform better, it's unlikely that performance will improve. It's that simple.

So, Effectiveness Enhancement generally involves starting from square one with each employee to define the details of how his or her performance should be managed. Management doesn't dictate the terms or determine the system. Rather, manager and individual employee work together to develop a single system for that employee. Employees doing the same job may end up being evaluated in completely different ways.

How to Design an Individualized System

The core of Effectiveness Enhancement is how it's developed. Here's a road map to follow if you would like to set up a completely individualized system or at least a more flexible system than the "one size fits all approach" so common in today's companies.

Step 1: Define your customers. First and foremost, view the employee as the main customer. However, you need to consider others, yourself included. After all, the system has to work for you, the manager, and perhaps for others. So, the first step is to define who needs what from the performance management system. Weigh employee needs highly, but consider your own requirements regarding things like knowing what's going on.

Step 2: Define needs. For each of the "customer groups" you define in Step 1, determine what they need to achieve their goals or the goals of the company. By "determine," we mean that you ask those customers. So if you identified the Personnel Department as a key customer, ask the staff what they need to do. Also ask them why, just in case you need to set priorities. Go to your employees as a group or individually and say, "Our way of working and communicating about performance should be aimed at helping you improve in an ongoing way. What do you need so that can happen? How often do you need to meet with me? How should we plan your job responsibilities? What do we need to do to prevent small problems from growing?"

> **Define "Customers"**
> Begin by answering these two questions:
> • Who are the people most likely to cause the system to fail or succeed?
> • Whose needs must be met to make the system work?
>
> **Smart Managing**

Step 3: Outline methods to meet the needs of your customers. Once you know what people need, you're in a position to negotiate, problem-solve, and develop a method that fits the bill. You do this with the "customers," so that what emerges is something you can all live with. If you're using different methods for different staff members, do a little "contract" that specifies your agreement about how performance is to be managed.

Step 4: Do it! Try it out.

Step 5: Evaluate it regularly. Whatever you end up doing, you must, absolutely must, evaluate whether it works in a dynamic, ongoing way. The key word with respect to Effectiveness Enhancement is flexibility.

Advantages of Effectiveness Enhancement

In addition to providing a flexible method for improving performance, basing the system on individual needs treats people as individuals who have different needs and requirements and who might benefit from different approaches. This fits well with the idea of empowering staff. It also allows for taking into account management needs or the needs of other stakeholders or customers for the process.

When done properly, involving staff in defining how performance is to be managed increases the buy-in on their part. Since they define it, it's theirs. That's really the key: it's not management doing it to employees, but employees working with management to design and own the system.

Disadvantages of Effectiveness Enhancement

Probably the biggest drawback of using individualized methods is that it seems strange. It's hard for people to get their heads around the idea that we can plan performance, communicate performance, and evaluate performance differently for Susan and Paul, even when Susan and Paul do the exact same job. Some human resources personnel simply won't tolerate it—it offends their notion of standardization. So, while it may be easier to get buy-in from your staff, it may be very difficult to get buy-in from other people in the organization who feel they need a common approach or structure.

The Bottom Line on Effectiveness Enhancement

Effectiveness Enhancement suits the reality of individual differences and individual needs. It helps employees own the process because they design it with the manager. It scares people who want a standard, "one size fits all" approach.

Here's a variation. If you aren't comfortable with using different approaches for different employees reporting to you, follow the steps we've outlined to create a single system that meets the needs of your employees as a group. In other words, work with those who report to you to define a little system that works for you and them. Or perhaps you might find, when discussing the issues with staff, that your administrative staff might need one method while your engineers might benefit from another.

The "Using Your Head No System System"

The term is a bit tongue-in-cheek. It's amusing but it reflects an interesting perspective. The best way to help you understand it is through a little story.

The story is told of a CEO of a manufacturing plant who decided to hit the floor. As he was walking around, he came across Ted, a machine operator, who was apparently doing nothing. The CEO approached Ted, asking him what was going on. The employee explained that he was waiting for a technician to come and recalibrate the equipment.

The CEO said, "Ted, help me understand this. How long have you worked on this machine?"

Ted replied, "Well, I guess about twenty years, sir."

Continuing, the CEO said, "Ted, are you telling me that after twenty years you don't know how to recalibrate the machine? That's hard to believe. I understand you may be the best machinist we have."

"Well, sir," Ted responded proudly, "I can tweak this baby with my eyes shut. But you see, recalibrating it isn't my job. My job description says that I am supposed to use the machine, and report calibration problems to the technician, but not to fix the machine. I don't want anyone getting upset."

Hiding his frustration, the CEO invited the machine operator into the office, asking him to bring a copy of the job description. "I'll tell you what," the CEO said, "we are going to write a completely new job description for you that makes a bit more sense." Without another word, the CEO tore up the job description and quickly wrote something down on a new sheet and handed it to Ted.

On the new job description was one sentence: "Use your head."

I don't know about you, but I love this story for its simplicity. What's the moral of the story? Perhaps it's that we can get things backward. Sometimes we forget that our purpose is to improve productivity and we actually create barriers to achieving that goal. Was the job description used intelligently here? No, it was stopping an employee from doing something within his power to get on with his work.

There's another moral to the story. The key to productivity and improvement is making sure that each and every employee understands the goals and purposes of the company, the division, and his or her own work unit and how he or she can best contribute

---

Smart Managing

How to Hit the Target

The core of the "use your head no system system" is that employees must understand their jobs and how they contribute to the overall success of the work group and the company. It's like an arrow. If you aim it right and release it carefully, it will hit the bull's-eye without any further guidance from you.

But whether you're using the "use your head" approach, a rating system, or even a dreaded ranking system, every performance management system requires that employees understand what they're doing and why within the "big picture."

toward achieving those goals. If employees have that knowledge, they become empowered to use their heads to make decisions. In fact, in so many instances, it's the employees who know what needs to be done and when it needs to be done.

In our complex work world, I can't counsel people to throw out their performance management systems and go to a "use your head" approach. It probably leaves employers open to lawsuits and grievances when disciplinary action is required. Still, it has an intuitive sense to it.

Manager's Checklist for Chapter 12

❑ Make your decision to try any of these performance management variations according to your situation, what everyone needs, and what you can get away with. Nobody can make the decision for you. Consider advantages and disadvantages carefully. Try to come up with ones not discussed here.

❑ As we've stressed throughout this book, no performance management system is perfect. Use your head. Decide what you need. Find out what other stakeholders need. Look at alternatives. Decide with other people which path to take. Finally, monitor any changes in your performance management system to assess whether things work better because of the changes and or whether additional changes are required.

❑ Bottom line, it's a dynamic process. Do it, test it, and change it if necessary.

Questions Managers Ask

We've covered a lot of ground so far. But one difficulty with books is you can't ask them questions and get answers. Most managers have a few questions about using performance management. Let's address the most common or important questions managers ask. You'll probably find some answers to questions that are going around in your head, too.

We'll address the following:

- How does performance management link up to rewards and pay for performance?
- How can performance management be used to empower staff?
- How do I work within a poorly designed system at my company?
- When staff set their own standards and targets, don't they set them too low?
- Don't employees tend to rate themselves too highly?
- I'm too busy. What do I do?
- What kinds of preparation do employees need to make this system work?

Links to Rewards and Pay for Performance

The question: My company is struggling to figure out a way to reward better performers with higher salaries, so we can encourage better performance and keep our staff more productive. It seems like there must be links between performance management and appraisal and pay for performance. Can you explain what those might be, indicate any pitfalls to avoid, and provide any other hints?

Linking performance management to pay for performance probably seems, on the surface, to be logical and sensible. After all, if you're already reviewing and somehow measuring performance and effectiveness, it makes sense to use that information for things like pay raises or promotions, doesn't it? It does seem sensible. But there are problems, which we need to discuss.

> **Be Alert**
>
> Most pay for individual performance schemes have positive effects and negative effects. Consider:
> - Pay for performance may motivate some and upset and anger others.
> - It's difficult to have a system that everyone agrees is fair.
> - Pay for performance tends to put manager and employee on opposite sides of the table, sometimes making it more difficult to work together.

The first thing your company needs to understand is that no way of measuring the value of any individual employee will be completely accurate or valid. Measurements and appraisals will always be open to dispute. If pay is not tied to something like seniority, appraisal disagreements between manager and employee may be a problem, but it will be small. But if you tie pay to appraisals, you have more riding on the outcome. Suddenly that disagreement becomes more serious and it's more likely manager and employee will end up in protracted wars. Tying pay to performance appraisals tends to put the manager and the employee on completely different sides: the manager tries to control spending, while the employee tries to get more money. The agenda shifts. It changes the dynamics and hurts the ability of manager and employee to work together to solve problems.

The second issue to address is whether your performance management and appraisal system is precise enough, valid enough, and fair enough to use to determine pay. If you use a rating system, or a ranking system, or even a 360-degree feedback system, you can be almost sure that it isn't going to fill the bill.

Ratings just aren't accurate enough or precise enough. They're too subjective and too easy to sway. A tricky employee can manipulate ratings somewhat. Why is that a concern? How about if you reward people who are undeserving or snub people who are deserving because your ratings are subjective and faulty? Imagine the anger and frustration.

More to the point, you may not be able to defend your pay decisions if there's a legal challenge. If a person accuses the company of arbitrarily denying him or her a raise, will a court accept your rating system as objective documentation that the complainant isn't deserving? Probably not.

One more concern. Are you comfortable with the idea that pay for performance may create side effects that you don't want? Here's the problem.

Smart Managing

Undesirable Side Effects

If you have a pay for individual performance system and you want to foster teamwork and team responsibility, you have a bit of a mismatch. You need to work really hard to create a sense of team when rewards systems are set up to encourage "star performance" more than teamwork.

Is it possible? Yes. Is it easy? No. Much will depend on your interpersonal and leadership skills.

Let's imagine you have a perfect way of assessing the degree to which each employee achieves his or her goals. You set standards, you measure, and you reward based on individual achievement. But there's a side effect. By creating a monetary incentive to hit some specific targets, you are, by exclusion, saying that things not tied to those targets aren't important. For example, you may encourage staff to act in cutthroat ways, avoid helping colleagues, or avoid important, necessary extra responsibilities that haven't been linked to pay for performance. In other words, you can create a situation where the forest gets lost for the trees and employees forget that their value comes not only from their individual successes, but also from their overall ability to contribute to the success of the team or the entire organization. You need to decide if you can live with that.

So, What to Do?

Acknowledge that no pay for performance system is perfect. Nor is there a perfect way of accurately assessing the value of employee contributions. So, is there a "best way"?

If you want to tie pay to performance, here's how to do it. You make it a part of the performance planning process. You establish the criteria for a pay increase when you set objectives and standards. So, at the beginning of the year, each employee should know what he or she needs to achieve in order to receive the pay increase or bonus. You don't tie pay to ratings or rankings. You make sure the criteria are as objective and measurable as possible to reduce arguments. And, finally, no surprises at the end of the year.

The key? Think of your managerial job as helping each employee hit that target, make that extra money, or get that promotion. Make it clear that you'll do what's necessary to help every employee succeed. That's the only way to do it. You could try to limit pay raises and play the salary guardian role. That puts you in an impossible situation: the only way you can limit salary increases is if your staff fail. Is that where you want to go? In any event, if that's the role you want, you might as well give up, because eventually you'll create such bad blood between yourself and your employees that your ability to manage will be seriously damaged.

As a final remark on the subject, companies have faced the pay for performance problem for decades. Every approach has advantages and disadvantages. Before establishing company policies on the matter, it may be a good idea to read about alternative methods for rewarding good performance. There are other ways, like gain sharing or tying rewards to team performance or the company's performance rather than only to individual performance. Sometimes a combination of reward systems works much better and has fewer nasty side effects than a single way of rewarding performance.

Performance Management and Staff Empowerment

The question: Our senior executives decided to empower staff and flatten the organization to reduce the number of middle managers and supervisors. Is performance management the way you've described it consistent with staff empowerment or in conflict with it?

The answer to your question is fairly straightforward. You can't empower staff without informing them, teaching them, and making sure they have the necessary knowledge to make good decisions on their own.

In fact, that's one reason why empowerment efforts fail. Executives get the idea that employees need to have more control, but don't give them the needed knowledge. Then, when staff make the wrong decisions (which they will if they lack needed information), managers and executives throw up their hands in frustration. They decide that empowerment doesn't work, often blame employees, and move back to a more autocratic approach. It can't succeed unless employees have the tools they need to succeed at exercising responsibility and power.

Performance management is a key tool in the process of making clear to staff what their jobs are and how the jobs link up to the company values, principles, and policies. That should occur naturally during performance planning.

There's more. Ongoing performance communication keeps employees on track, provides regular updates about changes employees need to consider in their work, and keeps everyone current. Finally, the ideal situation is to develop staff to the point where they can assess their own progress whether there's a manager around or not. Performance management is a way of engineering successful empowerment and successful decision making. That means less ongoing

"Doing to" vs. "Doing with"

The reason why some people believe that there's a conflict between performance management and empowerment is that they hold an old-fashioned view of performance management. By now it should be clear that if you think of performance management as something done to an employee, you won't be helping your staff become empowered. If you think of it as working with employees, then it integrates very well.

need for management involvement, which is pretty important when there are fewer middle managers.

Working within a Poor System

The question: My company uses a rating system, which, quite frankly, is a joke for most managers and employees. Some of us have tried to get things changed, but it's not going to happen. So how do you have any credibility with staff or do any good with performance management when you have to use something that employees consider a joke?

First, understand that your credibility comes from how you behave every day, what you say, and how you act with respect to your employees. If employees see you helping them succeed, they will be less concerned with the "bogus" forms. Here are some suggestions:

- Always keep in mind that performance management isn't about the form, but about establishing mutual understanding about what employees are expected to do and how you, as a manager, can help them do it. Keep sending that message to staff.
- If you focus on mutual understanding, you can indicate that you know the form or system isn't perfect. Life isn't

perfect. Damage to credibility occurs when managers pretend they're doing something useful when everyone knows it's not. Bottom line: you can add things to meet your needs and those of your staff, right?

- Don't pretend the forms are wonderful, if everyone knows they're terrible, but don't dwell on how useless the form might be. Focus on what you and your staff need to improve. Find solutions. Get staff involved in figuring out how to make it work.

Do Staff Set Low Standards for Themselves?

The question: I believe that staff should be actively involved in setting their own objectives and standards of performance or targets, and I want to move in that direction with my staff. My concern is that they will set standards too low so they'll look good at evaluation time. Any comments?

That isn't what usually happens. Why not? Research shows that most people feel they're above average in ability or contribution—which, by the way, is statistically impossible. What that means is that they feel quite competent and able. So, they tend to set their targets too high or take on too much because they believe in their abilities. The flip side is that when people rate themselves using rating scales, they tend to overrate themselves if the criteria are really vague.

That's the general explanation. You'll find many exceptions. You'll find people who have no confidence in their abilities. Also, there's no denying that some people are lazy and will set easy targets. Your role as a manager is to help them set realistic, achievable goals that require them to stretch a little. The nice thing about negotiating standards and targets is that, while you're encouraging staff to set standards that require stretching, you're also expressing your confidence and trust in the ability of the employees to achieve those goals. That's motivating. Offering to help staff hit those higher targets also puts you and the employees on the same side.

Unrealistic Employee Ratings

The question: Don't employees tend to rate themselves too highly?

Yes, as we mentioned in the answer to the previous question, if you ask people to rate themselves using some very vague, fuzzy criteria, they will tend to rate themselves as above average. For example, if you give the directions, "On a scale from poor to excellent (1 to 5), rate yourself in terms of your value as an employee," probably 80% of the employees will rate themselves as being above average. The more general and vague the rating item, the more likely this will happen.

The question touches on a primary fault of rating-based systems. The criteria are usually vague, and that leads to some difficult negotiations or arguments, sometimes ugly arguments. So, what's the solution?

Objectives Aren't That Objective Either

It's obvious that ratings are fairly subjective. What's less obvious is that more specific targets and standards of performance, which might seem very objective, are not. Understand that there can be disagreement about the meaning of objectives or whether an employee has met them. Your "evaluation" isn't going to be perfect, and neither is the employee's self-evaluation.

The reason targets and standards are more useful than rating systems is they're less open to bias in evaluation. Let's compare two methods, one based on a rating scale and the other based on an objective or target.

Imagine the following on a rating form:

Demonstrates and Applies Superior Selling Techniques

Never	Sometimes	Half the Time	Usually	Always

Where do you think most people will rate themselves? If you guessed "usually," you're right. Even inferior salespeople are going to rate themselves at that level.

Now, let's use a more objective target:

Objective: Increase sales by 10%

Standard: Objective will be met if salesperson sells $30,000 worth of product each quarter

Using the objective and the standard, the evaluation process is pretty simple. Either the salesperson hits the target or not. It doesn't matter if a salesperson could sell ice to penguins or couldn't sell gold at a dollar an ounce. What matters is to increase sales by 10% and sell $30,000. With an objectives- and standards-based system, you have fewer arguments resulting from different interpretations of rating scale items.

The "I'm Too Busy to Do It" Excuse

The question: I'm overworked and underpaid. I'm just too busy managing to be able to set aside the amount of time needed to do performance management as you describe it. What do I do?

Let me answer this with a question. Let's say you have an employee hired to assemble chairs. He comes to you and says, "Gee, you know, I'm sorry, but I'm so busy I don't have time to assemble all these chairs. I have meetings to attend and I help other people assemble their chairs and I'm not paid enough." How would you react? You'd probably answer, "Hey, what do you think we hired you to do? You are a chair maker. That's your job." That just makes sense.

So let's go back to the question. Managers are busy. But the question you need to ask yourself is, "What is my job?" If your answer is, "My job is to make sure my staff can do their jobs productively," then clearly performance management should be an area where you spend a good amount of your time. If you don't "have the time," you need to look at where your time is going, how it is allocated, and how you manage your priorities.

The reality is that many managers who claim they don't have time to fulfill their primary job function (help their staff succeed) are thinking about the process backward. They don't have the time because they micromanage, getting involved in all the little things that should be handled by others. They don't have the time because they fight forest fires gone out of control because of neglect. And they clean up messes rather than prevent them. That's why they don't have the time. So, consider the following points:

- Since the work that goes on in your department is the reason why your department exists, doesn't it make sense to make sure that getting the work done through other people becomes your highest priority?
- Identify where your time is going. Could you reduce the time you spend micromanaging or fighting forest fires by working with your staff and helping them do their jobs so you don't have to be involved in everything?
- Don't overestimate the time needed for good performance management. Yes, it takes time, but probably not as much time as you think. Apart from the performance planning and performance appraisal meetings, a good deal of the ongoing communication about performance, diagnosis of problems, and problem solving can be done in informal ways. I'd guess that most managers waste time doing the wrong things or unnecessary things. Reallocate that time to prevention and you may end up with more time.

Employee Preparation

The question: What kinds of preparation do employees need to make this system work?

That's an excellent question. Most companies, when they're introducing a performance management system, realize they need to train their managers and supervisors to use the system. Few companies understand that both managers and staff need to work together to make any system work. So

Smart Managing

Review Every Year

Don't assume that once you've prepared staff for performance management, they'll stay prepared forever. It's always a good idea to revisit things like why performance management is done and how, even if staff have been through it before.

employees as well as managers need to be prepared. Most companies don't do it or assume that the managers will prepare the employees.

So, what do employees need to understand, know, and be able to do so they can work with managers to improve performance using performance management? Pretty much the same things as managers.

For employees to become partners in the performance management process, they need to understand:

- The purpose of the performance management system in terms of the company and the work unit.
- How the performance management process will benefit them personally.
- The focus: preventing and solving problems, partnering between manager and employee, and creating success for everyone.

They may also need to develop the following skills:

- Communication and negotiation skills
- Skills in the nuts and bolts of writing clear objectives and clear standards of performance.

Tricks of the Trade

Explain in Detail with Narratives

Employees will be uneasy if they haven't taken part in a proper performance management process. One way of overcoming that feeling is to explain what kinds of dialogue will occur at the meetings. Explain the questions you'll be raising and what kinds of answers they might offer. Consider writing a little dialogue and sharing it with employees in advance, to give them a better feel for the process.

Finally, they need:

- An understanding of what will take place in the various meetings (performance planning, ongoing communication, and performance review meetings), so they'll feel less anxious about the process.

- A sense of the overall goals of the company and the work unit and how their job responsibilities fit into them.

Methods for Preparing and Educating Staff

There are various ways to educate and prepare staff for the performance management process. The primary and most powerful techniques lie with you, the manager. Why? Because each manager will have a slightly different approach or perspective on the process. Staff need to know what you think and how you are going to do things, not the company line.

Here are some options:

- Before you begin the performance management cycle (i.e., before meeting with staff to plan performance), hold a general staff meeting to review the purpose, the benefits, and what to expect. At this point, you can also ask the question, "For those of you who have done this with me before, do you have any suggestions about how we could improve the process this year?" That helps staff feel that the process is a partnership.
- Make sure staff have any written materials they require for the process (e.g., summary of work unit goals and objectives for the year, job descriptions).
- As a starting point in performance planning and performance appraisal meetings, explain the process briefly and ask: "Before we get into it, do you have any questions about what we're going to do?"
- If you're using a ratings form, go over it with staff beforehand and explain what you think each item means. If you're using objectives and standards, you'll need to coach staff on writing standards that are clear.

Are there other components useful in preparing staff? Yes. Some companies include details about their performance management system as part of employee orientation. So, all new employees have the system explained to them early on in their employment. Also, if you plan on using an objectives-and standards-based system, it's not a bad idea to provide training to staff on how to write proper objectives and standards. Corporate training departments can help identify or supply this kind of training.

Manager's Checklist for Chapter 13

❑ Performance management and pay for performance can be linked. Be aware that linking the two changes the dynamics of performance management and the relationship between you and your employees. Keep in mind what you gain and what you may lose.

❑ Performance management (or the information exchanged as part of performance management) is a key part of employee empowerment. It enables employees to make good decisions based on sound information.

❑ Poor performance management systems abound. If you're stuck with one, focus on building relationships with staff and supplement what you "must" do with what you and your employees find useful. You can succeed in spite of a poor system.

❑ Employees tend to set high standards for themselves. However, when using vague ratings, they also tend to rate themselves as above average.

❑ If you feel you're too busy to invest the time in performance management, ask yourself what your most important job responsibility might be. Examine your priorities and consider whether investing the time to prevent problems may give you more time, not less.

❑ Both you, as a manager, and your employees need to be prepared for performance management. Educate your staff. The more they understand, the more comfortable and less anxious they will be.

People Process, People Techniques

As we come to the end of this book, it's time to swing the spotlight to a central theme of this book—that performance management works according to the ability of the manager to establish positive relationships with employees, so that employees and manager can work as partners. It's a people process that requires the manager to have strong interpersonal skills.

In my consulting work, I've talked with thousands of employees and managers in many organizations. Over ten years I've never seen a performance management system work where the manager had poor interpersonal skills. Never! No system, no level of technical expertise in using forms or establishing objectives can make up for poor relationships between manager and employee. On the other hand, I've seen managers succeed with no formal performance management system or a horribly designed one. How? They use effective communication skills and an ability to work with employees and put employees and manager on the same team.

It's fitting that we look at the people process and the people techniques needed to make performance management work. In this chapter, we'll look at the mind-set of managers who succeed at performance management. What do they believe about employees? What do they believe about their own jobs? We'll also look at some of the basic people techniques required to succeed, not only at performance management but at management in general.

Your People Mind-set

Throughout this book we've focused on the performance management process as a people process. What you do is influenced by how you see yourself and your employees. For example, if you see yourself as an "imperial manager," someone who commands, that will affect your ability to work with employees. If you think employees are lazy, that too will influence your behavior. Whether accurate or not, your mind-set will affect your success in performance management. Let's list what we think are the essential assumptions of successful managers and successful performance managers.

The Success Mind-set

Successful performance managers tend to act on the following six assumptions.
- Performance management is a process undertaken *with* employees and not done *to* employees.
- Except for unusual situations that require unilateral disciplinary action, the planning, communicating, and evaluating of performance occur as a partnership.
- Most employees, once they understand what's required of them, will make every effort to meet those requirements.
- The purpose of performance management isn't to look at the past and assign blame for mistakes but to solve performance problems as they occur and prevent them whenever possible.
- When performance deficits occur, we need to identify the real causes of the deficit, whether they are causes in the system or causes connected with the individual employee.
- For the most part, if the manager does his or her job in

supporting employees, each employee is really the "resident expert" about the job he or she does and how to improve performance.

These six beliefs or assumptions are basic to successful performance management. Without that perspective, the process of performance management becomes confrontational and impossible. Adopt the successful mind-set and you can begin to change what goes on in performance discussions and change how employees and managers perceive the process.

> ### Consistent Communication
> **TRICKS OF THE TRADE**
>
> Your relationship with employees isn't defined just by what you do when discussing performance. It comes from how you interact with them each and every day. The more skilled, positive, and consistent your communication, the easier it will be to involve employees in performance management.

Essential Interpersonal Skills

If your beliefs and assumptions about your job and about your employees serve as the foundation for your performance management house, interpersonal techniques are the beams and supports that hold up the house. Many a well-designed performance management system has failed in the hands of unskilled managers. Many a poorly designed system can be made to succeed in the hands of a skilled manager.

To some people the term "interpersonal techniques" sounds somehow mushy or "touchy-feely." But interpersonal skills are really no different from any other kinds of skills. Interpersonal skills enable you to interact with people effectively. That means building positive relationships with enough rapport to communicate openly so problems can get solved. Acquiring and applying interpersonal skills allow you to get where you want to go most efficiently.

Before we discuss these "interpersonal skills" with respect

to performance management, we need to make one very important point. The relationships you need to have with employees to make performance management work aren't created (or destroyed) only during the performance management process. They are created and re-created on a daily basis. You may be the best communicator in the land during performance management discussions, but if you act like a jerk the rest of the time you'll hurt the relationships you need. Staff will be uncomfortable, mistrustful, and wary, and that's not going to encourage them to discuss their performance with you honestly and openly. To make performance management work, managers need to use effective interpersonal and communication skills all the time.

Climate-Setting Skills

By now you understand that performance management works best when manager and employee engage in the process willingly because they both understand the process and how each benefits from doing so. While they share the responsibility for making performance management work, it falls to the manag-

---

The Self-Destructing Manager

Jack was a manager who maintained a fairly good relationship with his employees. He believed in working with them, involving them in decision making, and he built cooperative relationships. But, within an hour, he undid it all.

At a staff meeting, he seemed to "lose it" for no reason. In a sudden outburst, he went from employee to employee, swearing and expressing his personal frustration with each of them. They sat in shocked silence as Jack destroyed their trust in him. What's worse, nobody dared to broach the subject with Jack for fear he'd unload on them again. After that incident, staff were no longer willing to discuss their performance openly and honestly with a manager who was so unpredictable. The outcome? Jack moved from a participatory form of management to an autocratic one. Not surprising. His staff weren't as interested in being involved anymore.

er to lead or guide the process and to create an understanding of the process that puts the employee at ease. This is critical, whether we're talking about performance planning meetings, ongoing communication, or the appraisal meeting.

Creating Clarity of Purpose

As part of any formal discussion of performance (particularly during planning and appraisal), it's important to refocus the employee on the reasons for meeting and what the outcomes should be. That gives you the opportunity to stress the basic principles you'll be following and helps to reassure staff.

Here's a way of doing it:

"Mark, I know this is our third go-around at performance planning, but let's go over why we're doing this. The major purpose is to come to some agreement about your job tasks and responsibilities so we are both on the same wavelength about what you should be doing and where you should be allocating your time. By the time we've finished, you and I will be in agreement about [topic areas]. We'll also produce a list of responsibilities on paper, which we will both sign, and we'll use that document during the year to gauge your progress. That's how I see it going. Is there anything else you would like to accomplish through this process or anything that would make it more useful to you?"

> **Don't Assume Understanding**
>
> Many employees have had bad experiences discussing their performance with managers. That can make them anxious even if their experiences with you have been positive. For that reason, don't assume that employees are comfortable or remember the purpose of the process. Be prepared to establish the purpose, a sense of joint responsibility, and a helping relationship at each step in the process.

Creating Joint Responsibility

In an earlier chapter, we mentioned that one cause of performance management failure is that the manager believes that it's the responsibility of the employee alone to improve his or her performance. That fosters a climate of blame and puts the employee on the defensive. It's important, early on in any performance discussion, to make it clear that you and the employee share that responsibility and to reassure him or her.

For example:

"Mark, let me tell you how I see my role here. First, my job is to help you get your job done and to guide us so we come to some mutual understanding of your job. So in our discussions we are both going to be responsible for making sure we understand each other, and we both need to work together so you can do your job as well as you can with a minimum of hassles. And my job is also to try to clear out obstacles. On the other side, you are probably the expert in your job, so I'm looking to you to identify problems you've encountered and come up with possible solutions so you can work more effectively. Does that make sense?"

Make It Interactive

When you set the scene, emphasize "we," to stress that the process depends on a partnership of manager and employee. Also use questions early on, to establish a dialogue, to elicit responses and suggestions. So much of the success of performance discussions depends on the setting. Create an interactive climate by involving staff in a dialogue.

Clarifying Process

With respect to performance discussions, employees are anxious about two things: why the discussion is taking place and how the discussion will go. We've stressed the need to clarify the purpose. You also need to clarify what's going to happen.

Here's a sample explanation:

"Mark, I've explained the purpose of our meeting and where we need to end up. Here's what I see us doing. Please make suggestions or changes that you might find helpful. We're going to begin by looking at the goals of the company and our own unit. Next, we'll go over your job description to see if it still makes sense. Then we need to identify the five or six most important parts of your job and figure out how we can both know when you've succeeded in completing those tasks. Rather than telling you, I'm going to be asking questions of you, because you've been doing your job for five years and know a whole lot more about it than I do."

Conflict Prevention Skills

Let's begin by clarifying what we mean by "conflict prevention skills." Conflict or disagreement, by itself, need not be a big problem. Some of the best solutions come when two people disagree and then work it out together. What we need to be concerned about are conflicts or disagreements that are unnecessary or

Start with Personal Responsibility

To prevent conflict, begin by outlining your responsibilities as a manager. Then move on to stating what you need from the employee to make the process work. Create a helping relationship, a partnership. Avoid anything that suggests "I tell you and you do what I say."

come about through the use of language and tone that tend to cause irrelevant and sidetracking conflict. Many people talk about "personality conflicts," but that's really not the right term for these unnecessary conflicts. They're really language or tone conflicts—conflicts resulting from an antagonistic manner.

Let's briefly look at some types of conflict-provoking language and how you can instead use language that promotes cooperation and is less likely to create bad feelings. You want to avoid provoking conflicts, not only during interactions about performance, but in every interaction you have in the workplace.

Invite Involvement

Explicitly and up front, invite the employee to make suggestions. Although you have a sense of what's going to happen during the discussion, keep the process flexible so it meets the needs of the employee as well. Even if you have a map for the process, encourage staff to modify that map when and if it doesn't make sense.

Person-Centered Comments and Criticism

Comments and criticism can cause conflicts when they target a person and his or her general behavior, rather than focusing on a specific problem. For example:

- You aren't listening.
- You don't know what you are talking about.
- Who are you to tell me...?
- Can't you just be quiet for a minute?
- Have you even read the report?

Comments and questions like these sound like accusations, rather than attempts to help. They interfere with problem solving. It doesn't matter whether or not they're true; they are still destructive. Stick to the real issues.

Past-Centered Comments

While it's legitimate to talk about what has happened in the past, particularly when reviewing performance, it's not appropriate to use past mistakes to bludgeon staff. The only reason to look in the rearview mirror is to prevent problems from recurring—not to embarrass or humiliate.

Avoid past-centered comments that serve no purpose:

- We tried that and it didn't work.
- For years, you've been late getting your work done.
- If I had a nickel for every time you've been late in your career, I'd be able to retire.

Guilt-Induction Attempts

Some managers believe that if they make employees feel guilty, they'll work harder. Usually such attempts backfire because the employees feel manipulated. Here are some examples of guilt induction that should be avoided.

- If you really cared about this team, you would work harder.
- Most of you seem to be trying really hard to make this fail.
- I guess you don't care much about this project.
- I work so hard and you don't seem to appreciate all my work on your behalf.

Inappropriate Reassurance and Positive Thinking

Not all conflict-provoking language is critical or negative. Some actually sounds helpful—but it can still cause problems. When talking about a performance problem, a manager might try to reassure the employee that he or she will be able to overcome the difficulty. Even if the manager intends to convey confidence, the reassurance might not be helpful in itself, because it doesn't explain how this is going to happen or how the manager is going to help.

Look at the following hollow attempts at reassurance:

- I know the project is late, but I'm sure somehow you will catch up.
- Things are rough now, but you'll get a handle on them.
- I know you feel like you don't know how to do this, but you'll get it.
- You'll do fine, you'll see.

Sometimes it's OK to reassure, but it's far better to reassure while working with the employee to solve the problem.

Unsolicited Advice and Commands

As a manager you have the right to provide advice and even, occasionally, to order people to do things. That doesn't mean you should rely on that right. When you provide unsolicited advice, you give the impression that you feel superior to the employee, which can embarrass him or her, particularly if you offer that advice publicly. Also, if you're in the habit of ordering people around, then it will be very difficult to switch from the boss role to the partner role, which is really a necessity for performance management. Some examples to avoid:

It Works Both Ways

Smart Managing

We're focusing on your use of conflict-prevention techniques. But if you really want a great payoff, help your employees learn to prevent conflict, negotiate fairly, and treat people (you, customers, and colleagues) with respect. There are training courses for these skills. When you and your employees both use them, it makes performance management much easier.

- You must do it this way.
- Photocopy this and give me a copy.
- This is the only way to do it.
- Get this done today and leave it on my desk.

You're better off using a more cooperative tone, asking rather than telling. If you feel the need to provide advice (and it's not an emergency situation), consider asking first. For example: "I know of another way you might be able to get this done that might be easier for you. Do you want to hear it?"

Aggressive Questions

Questions are critical to involve employees, not only in performance management discussions, but also in any other aspects of your work. But some people use questions to express disdain, to attack, or to belittle.

For example:

- Why in the world would you say that?
- Would you be so kind as to defend your position?
- What makes you think that...?
- How in the world did you come to that conclusion?

Can you see how these questions could make someone defensive, particularly if you use them with an annoyed or disdainful tone? Be careful to rephrase to sound more cooperative.

Try something like "I'm not sure I understand what you are saying. Could you explain a bit more?" or "Maybe you have a really good idea here, but I'm not getting it. Could you explain why you believe that...?"

> ### Individualize Your Communication
>
> We've warned about ways of communicating that can be problematic. All people are different. There may be some staff who need constant encouragement...or may even need to be pushed daily to do well. Individualize how you communicate with each employee according to his or her needs. To do that, you must be observant about the effects of your behavior on the other person.

Statements of Mistrust

Managers, in a misguided attempt to get commitment from an employee, will say things that can be quite insulting because they suggest that the manager doesn't trust him or her. For example:

- Are you sure that you will have this in on time?
- I've heard you say that before.

Such comments imply mistrust, which only undermines your partnership. Don't express doubt, but rather work toward a position that you can more readily believe.

Imagine, for example, that you're planning performance with an employee. She wants to commit to a time schedule you don't see as realistic or practical. Don't ask doubtfully, "Are you sure you'll have this in on time?" Seek a compromise: "I think it's important that we plan enough time to get this done so we can be sure you're not rushed or pressured. Can we consider changing that time line to give you a bit of breathing room? Then, if you beat the deadline, that's great."

Overstatements

Avoid phrasings that exaggerate, often with such words as *always, never,* and *every time.* Overstatements usually result in arguments because most overstatements are inaccurate. When you exaggerate your point, it rarely strengthens it, because you're stretching it beyond the truth. Also, employees feel they have to defend themselves against what they perceive as an unfair attack. Some examples:

- You never get your work in on time.
- Every time I've asked you to do X, you mess it up.
- You always try to avoid accepting advice from me.

Avoid overstatements. Use more precise statements that are oriented toward solutions. For example: "John, we've had three situations where your projects have come in late, so I'd like to work with you to identify where the barriers lie and what we can do about them. Let's talk first about the Aardvark project."

Notice the difference. The overstatements are accusatory—and probably untrue. It's far more effective to define the problem precisely and to focus on solving it as partners.

Defusing Skills: When Things Get Heated

I'd love to tell you that you will never have disagreements with employees during the performance management process. But that would be a lie.

Even if you establish positive relationships with your employees and work to prevent conflict, sooner or later disagreements will happen. But performance management disagreements need not poison your relationships with staff with whom you disagree. It all depends on how you handle the conflict and how you resolve it. In fact, out of some performance-related disagreements come some of the best solutions to performance problems.

Here are some suggestions for cooling down situations that are getting too hot:

- When conflicts occur during performance-related discussions, focus on two goals. First, you need to come to some agreement on the issue. It's not a question of who will win, but of finding a mutually acceptable position. Second, whatever the subject, manage the discussion so it's less likely to hurt your relationship and cause future performance problems. Both goals are important.
- Allow some room for the employee to express frustration and anger without firing back. Sometimes people say things that they don't mean when they're frustrated.
- Remember that conflict occurs when people care about what they do. Think of conflict about performance as a conversation between two people who care a lot about the discussion. That helps you keep a positive attitude.
- You have two options for handling conflict. You can attempt to win the battle by persuading, exerting pressure, or using power for leverage. Or, you can first try to understand the employee's position and then work toward a solution. The first option is more likely to polarize the situa-

tion and cause further problems. So, work to understand the employee first and then find a solution. That's the battle that really matters—and both of you can win.

- One of the most powerful techniques for dealing with disagreements is active listening. Active listening involves paraphrasing what the other person has said so you prove that you've understood his or her point of view. That builds bridges and helps the other person slow down and start listening to you.

- A basic principle to apply when dealing with an upset or angry employee is to focus first on his or her feelings. The reason is simple. Angry people are not good at solving problems. First, the emotional energy has to vent. One powerful technique to use is empathy. If you're dealing with someone who's upset, acknowledge the feelings being expressed, rather than trying to solve the problem. For example, "It sounds like you are upset that we disagree about whether you hit your target."

- When disagreements occur, it's easy to get distracted from the real issue, which is coming up with some solution to solve the problem or disagreement. Stay on the issue and away from personal remarks, blaming remarks, or comments you might make in frustration or anger. In other words, adopt a solution-oriented approach. It's not about winning or humiliating or being right. It's about finding a solution.

- There may be times during communication about performance where one or both of you will be sufficiently upset that constructive dialogue becomes impossible. Be alert for those times. If you feel the emotional levels are too intense, take a time-out. In a meeting, this might mean taking five minutes to get some coffee or a breath of fresh air. In more intense situations, you may want to stop the discussion and come back to it when both of you are calmer. Here's a phrase to use: "I think both of us are getting pretty intense about this, so maybe now is not the best time to finish this conversation. Why don't we leave it for today? We can come back to this tomorrow after we've both had time to think about how we might come to some agreement, OK?"

Manager's Checklist for Chapter 14

❏ To make performance management work, you need to adopt certain assumptions that foster a spirit of partnership and cooperation.

❏ Think about the ways you communicate and interact with staff, both during performance discussions and in other situations. If you think they dislike talking with you, if they're uneasy or anxious, if you get the sense they keep bad news from you, then try to identify the reasons. In the spirit of becoming a better manager, ask your staff, "Are there things that I do or say that make you feel uncomfortable talking with me?"

❏ Try to eliminate conflict-provoking behaviors from your communication. Employees will trust you more—although it sometimes takes a long time—and it will be easier to work together to manage performance.

❏ You can function as a communication role model. Your staff will take some of their cues from you. If you prevent unnecessary conflict, if you treat them in positive ways, they're more likely to learn how to do so. Don't underestimate your ability to teach and coach staff so they too can learn to use more effective interpersonal techniques.

Performance Management in Action

Now that we've covered the principles and process of performance management, what would it look like in action? Remember the story that opened Chapter 1, about Michael and the Acme Progressive Company? Michael wasn't managing performance with the fourteen staff members who reported to him. Whatever he did probably hurt more than helped. Well, something happened to Michael while you were reading this book.

He got a new boss. Marie was hired from outside Acme to help get the company on track. Tough, supportive, and talented, she decided things were all too chaotic and it was time to take action.

The First Step toward Improving Performance Management

At the end of June, Marie asked Michael to schedule a meeting with her to discuss the performance of his department. After some preliminary chitchat, Marie got to the point: "Michael, I've been looking at the performance of all the departments in my division and I'm really concerned. We're going backward, and we need to turn it around or Acme is going to be in big trouble. I need to know from you what you think the problem is with your group."

After some thought, Michael replied: "I know productivity seems to be down, but it's like we have more and more work and less and less time. My staff is getting worn down and they seem to be making a lot more mistakes. Frankly, we could do with more staff."

Marie shook her head slowly, and then explained that, because of Acme's financial situation, staffing levels had been frozen. Then she continued: "I know you're really busy, but 'busy' isn't the point, is it? Everyone may be working hard, but is it possible that they may not be focusing on the really important things they need to do to get productivity up?"

"It's interesting you bring that up," Michael replied. "It looks to me like people are forgetting what's important and not so important. In fact, we seem to be spinning our wheels."

"Good," Marie said. "That's my impression also. How are you working with staff to keep them focused on the important work and making sure it gets done effi-

---

TRICKS OF THE TRADE

Diagnosis and Cooperation

Notice that Marie isn't telling Michael what to do. She's working with him, asking questions to try to uncover the underlying problem. That's part of diagnosis, whether it's during performance planning or performance appraisal. The goal is to identify barriers to achievement and overcome them together.

---

ciently? How are you managing their performance?"

Michael paused for a moment, looking a bit embarrassed, and then answered: "Well, you know I'm pretty busy. But we have meetings every two months to talk about the work and we do that once-a-year thing that the personnel department forces us to do—you know, with those forms to fill out?"

"I know about those forms," Marie sighed. "They make me turn them in too."

She paused, and then continued: "That's not enough. We need to do something here to help you and your staff or there are going to be some serious shake-ups.

"Here's what we're going to do. I'd like you to start managing performance with your staff—and it's got to be meaningful. But it's not something you have to do on your own. I'll be doing the same things with all my managers. So, while I'm helping you with your performance, you'll be using the same techniques to help your staff.

"Here's how we're going to start. The vice presidents have set a number of goals and objectives for the company for the next year. Each department is expected to contribute to achieving those goals. In about a year you and I are going to sit down and assess whether your department has met that obligation. As the manager, I expect you to be accountable and responsible for making sure it happens."

Michael, looking a bit green, said: "Well, OK, I guess that's why I get paid the big bucks. How are you going to measure this? Not with that horrible ratings form, I hope?"

"No," Marie answered

> ### Cascade Down
>
> If you have supervisors who report to you, you will want to manage their performance in the same way you want them to manage the performance of their staffs. Model the process, teach it by your example, and support your managers in their performance management efforts.
>
> **TRICKS OF THE TRADE**

quickly. "You and I are going to talk and set objectives for you personally. That's what we'll measure. Those measures need to be simple and possible to measure. And we'll develop them together, but mostly you will be suggesting them, since you know your job best."

"And I guess you want me to do the same thing for my staff?"

"Exactly." Marie nodded energetically. "That's how we'll coordinate the company's goals with your department's goals and the objectives for your staff. We'll still have to complete those ratings forms, but I've talked to personnel and they've

Stuck with a Poor Form?

TRICKS OF THE TRADE

No good manager simply accepts a bad system! If you're required to use flawed forms, augment them with something that works. Then, work to change the system. The most effective argument? The success of your approach to performance management.

agreed, for now, to let you add some notes to them. Maybe next year we can convince them to drop the ratings entirely."

Michael felt ready to deal with specifics, so Marie closed the meeting by scheduling another.

"What I'd like you to do," she said, "is take the goals and objectives for the whole company and discuss them with your staff. You and I will get together again in about three weeks to set your department's goals and your personal objectives and standards, which we'll use to assess your progress at the end of the year. Then, you're going to do something similar with your staff, and you will measure and manage their performance the same way." She paused. "What do you think?"

"I'm not sure I have much choice," Michael admitted, "but I'll give it a try."

After a little more discussion, Marie gave Michael some material on performance management and writing objectives and standards. Then they scheduled their next meeting.

Michael reviewed the overall goals for the company, and then called a staff meeting. At that meeting, he ex-

Involve Staff in the Big Picture

Smart Managing

It's important that staff understand how they fit in with the success of their department and with the whole organization. By involving staff in determining the best way to contribute to the overall goals, you can make their jobs mean more to them.

plained that employees needed to link their individual performance to achieve the goals set for the organization. They all discussed what they would need to do and came up with a set of goals and objectives for the department.

Michael closed the meeting by explaining what was to happen next: "I'm taking our goals up to Marie to make sure she feels we're aiming at the right bull's-eye. They might change a bit, but I think we have them pretty well nailed down. After speaking with Marie, I want to schedule a meeting with each one of you to discuss how your work in the next year is going to tie into our overall goals. At that time, we'll decide how to keep track of progress and determine how we're going to evaluate your work against those objectives."

Agreeing on Goals and Objectives

About three weeks later, Marie and Michael met again. They went over the goals and objectives set for the department and finalized them so they aligned with those of the company.

Then Marie summed up the results. "OK, Michael, now these are the things we've agreed that you and your department are going to achieve. You need to increase your sales by 10%, which seems a realistic goal. We need to limit errors in the ordering system, with our starting goal being one error a month. Also, we want to cut by 50% justified customer complaints going to the customer service department."

She paused and looked at Michael. He nodded slowly in agreement. Marie moved on.

"One more thing we've agreed upon is that the only way we can achieve these goals is if you carry out your managerial responsibilities regarding performance management with your staff. Now, since these are the criteria we're going to use to evaluate your performance, we need to be sure about them. Are those goals clear to you? Do they make sense? Will they get us where we need to go?"

Michael was a bit concerned. "What happens to me when we do our appraisal and I fall short? I don't know if I can control all these things."

"Good question." Marie replied. "OK, here's how we'll work it. Once a month you and I will meet for about fifteen minutes to discuss progress toward those goals and objectives. If it happens that we aren't making progress, then we'll figure out how to overcome any obstacles. If necessary we'll include your staff. OK?"

Michael nodded.

"My job is to help you do your job," Marie said, "and your job is to help your staff do theirs. Frankly, I'm not concerned that you won't meet the objectives, because together we can do and will do it. But, to answer your question, I won't be concerned if we miss those targets by a bit, provided we continue to improve. If we don't improve at all, then we'll have to take action, depending on why we haven't. You and I will look at our successes and any failures at your year-end performance review meeting. Then, we'll figure out where to go from there."

At the end of the meeting, Marie and Michael listed the objectives and standards that would be used to evaluate Michael and his department. To record their agreement, they had the objectives and standards typed up on a single sheet of paper, and had two copies made. Each signed both copies and kept one.

Planning Performance with Staff

In August, Michael met with each employee as Marie had met with him, to establish what each employee should do to contribute to the department's success and to agree on the standards for reviewing each employee's performance. Rather than establish standards himself, Michael asked each person to set them.

For example, this is how he handled that matter with Sarah, the receptionist and switchboard operator:

Smart Managing

Simple Documentation

To make sure both manager and employee are in agreement, and for legal reasons, it's important to document objectives and standards. You can do this as simply as possible, listing only the most important things to focus on. It's as important to document what happens in performance planning as it is to document what happens in the performance appraisal stage.

"Since we're concerned about customer service, we should decide on what would be the maximum number of rings for any phone call. What would you recommend?"

"Well," Sarah answered slowly, "I don't know."

"Would fifty rings be reasonable?"

"No," she laughed. "That would be much too long."

"Well," Michael asked, "how about two rings?"

"No, that's impossible—not practical."

Michael and Sarah continued back and forth, until eventually they agreed on a target of five rings. They decided to allow some leeway, agreeing that 95% of phone calls should be answered within five rings and that no call should ever ring more than fifteen times, under any circumstances. They thought this reasonable maximum would greatly reduce complaints about poor phone service.

Before they moved on to the next objective and standard, Michael asked: "OK, now, here's the key question. What do you need to be able to meet that standard? What can I do to help?" Sarah suggested a few small changes regarding phone coverage during coffee breaks and lunch and recommended buying a low-cost cordless headset so she could answer the phone even if she were away from her desk.

At the end of the meeting, Michael and Sarah followed the simple documentation process, recording the tasks, objectives, and standards they'd agreed upon.

By the end of August, Michael had met with each staff member, clarified jobs and standards, and identified some small, inexpensive changes they could make to help meet their objectives. In the process, he discovered a few things.

First, he realized that there were a lot of little obstacles and annoyances interfering with productivity—interferences they could remove or minimize themselves with little investment. Second, he found that once staff understood that he was there to help them do their jobs, not to beat them, they were cooperative, even happy with the process. Several times, at the end of meetings, employees even asked why Acme had waited so long before starting performance management.

Communicating about Progress and Solving Problems

During the year, Michael met regularly with employees to review their progress. Each month, in ten-minute, one-on-one meetings, he and each employee addressed two questions:

- How are you progressing in meeting your goals?
- What problems are you encountering?

In some cases, Michael made some notes on difficulties encountered. Sometimes a staff member needed to upgrade his or her skills, so Michael provided training and coaching. As time went on, he

Tricks of the Trade

Dynamic Goals and Standards
Never etch your goals and standards in stone. Be flexible enough on an individual basis so the department can react to company shifts. Progress meetings are a good place to examine whether any changes are needed.

found it necessary to change some of the objectives and standards, because the company had altered some of its priorities. Sometimes responsibilities shifted around; some were added and some were eliminated. After each series of regular meetings with his staff, Michael met with Marie, to update his boss and discuss his responsibilities with her as each of his employees had done with him.

Preparing for the Yearly Review

March 31 marked the end of Acme Progressive's fiscal year. One of Michael's responsibilities was to do a year-end performance review with each of his staff members. Since Michael knew he was going to be evaluated on those reviews, he felt motivated. Here's how he handled the reviews.

At a general staff meeting in late February, Michael reminded all of his employees that it was time to schedule meetings to discuss the past year's performance and plan for performance for the next year.

"As you all know, we've been working on improving our overall performance and meeting regularly to do that. It looks to me as if we've succeeded in clearing out some barriers and meeting our departmental goals. What we need to do next is discuss problems you faced in meeting your individual objectives and decide where we need to go for the next year.

"Since I've been meeting regularly with you, I don't expect any surprises, for you or for me. You all know where you stand, so we just need to do some paperwork and plan. I'd like you to look at the performance planning notes we made in our individual meetings and any other notes you might have from our regular progress meetings.

"When I meet with each of you, I'm going to ask you whether you feel you've hit the targets we set together and, just as we have done in our progress meetings, we'll look to remove future barriers. We'll make some notes and each of us will sign them. Of course, we'll also complete that rating form required for personnel. But we'll focus on the goals we negotiated."

Reviewing and Evaluating

In March, Michael met with each employee. He tried to speak very little, be as helpful as possible, and encourage the employee to evaluate his or her progress. For the most part, it worked well. There were no surprises for anyone.

In one instance, however, there was a problem. Fred had consistently missed the targets he'd set with Michael. Because Fred and Michael had been meeting regularly, both were anticipating a problem. How did Michael handle this?

First, he and Fred established that there was indeed a performance gap. Michael had kept notes on the problems from the progress meetings, so he had some data. He then started a diagnostic process to determine what had been causing the problem, as they'd done in their monthly meetings. They then agreed that Michael would continue to coach Fred.

Although Michael was generally supportive, he had to make sure Fred understood that both he and the company were serious about meeting performance goals.

Here's what he said:

"Fred, I'll continue to work with you. You've met some of your objectives and sometimes even surpassed what we asked of you. That tells me you have the ability to meet the rest of them in the new year. So, please come to me if you have any difficulties, and we'll continue to meet regularly. It might be, though, that you would be more successful in a job that builds on your strengths: that's something you and I need to look at if you miss your targets in the next quarter.

"So we don't lose sight of the issues, I've made some notes outlining our course of action. We'll both sign this paper, but I'm going to hold onto it for another three months. If you hit your interim targets for the next quarter and the next year, then I'll destroy the notes. If you miss your targets, the notes and documentation will go into your personnel file, and we'll need to figure out what to do next."

Fred reluctantly agreed.

The Outcomes

How does the story end? In fact, it never ends. The performance management process begins anew: the appraisals not only end the year but also begin the planning process for the next year. Let's summarize the outcomes.

Michael and his boss, Marie, met to do his appraisal. The results were good, although not news. Michael's department and Michael had met or surpassed all the goals. Marie and Michael were so pleased with the positive results that they met with the vice president of human resources to discuss their success and ask that everyone at Acme be given more flexibility. Personnel finally got rid of the required ratings forms.

Clearly the policy of "no surprises" worked well. Michael and his staff identified barriers early on and overcame most of them. Employees knew where they stood during the year and Michael had the information he needed. On a corporate level, everyone benefited by the linking of individual and departmental objectives to the overall goals of the company.

What about Fred? In a perfect world, Fred would have met his next year's objectives. Unfortunately, Fred continued to struggle, despite everyone's efforts to help. Eventually Michael decided to meet with Fred and the personnel department to see if another job at Acme would be more suitable. That way, the company could salvage its investment in Fred (the cost of hiring, training, etc.). Fred then chose to move (with great relief) to another position, where he could succeed. Could Acme have let Fred go? Yes, the firm had sufficient documentation to support that option—as a last resort.

Closing Comments

Performance management is, in some ways, very simple and, in other ways, very complex. It consists of lots of parts and it requires some skills. But if you approach it with the proper mind-set, you can make it work—and pay great benefits.

Manager's Checklist for Chapter 15

❑ Performance management is about people, communication, dialogue, and working together, not about forms or forcing employees to produce.

❏ Performance management is an ongoing process through-out the year. It's not just about performance appraisal. In fact, performance appraisal is only a small part of it.

❏ Performance management is about preventing and solving problems, not about punishing or blaming. By identifying problems and their causes as you go, you can work with staff to solve them.

❏ Aim at "no surprises." There shouldn't be any surprises for staff during appraisals and there should be no surprises for you regarding their progress.

Index

U

About the Author

Robert Bacal is head of two companies, Bacal & Associates, a training and consulting firm, and the Institute For Cooperative Communication, a virtual company whose mission is to research and develop instructional materials and to teach people how to communicate in more effective, harmonious ways in the workplace and at home. He holds a graduate degree in applied psychology and has been teaching, training, providing consulting services, and writing on workplace issues for twenty years. You can visit his Web site at http://www.escape.ca/~rbacal/.